Python for Kids: Fun Projects to Learn Programming

A Beginner's Guide to Coding, Games, and More

Greyson Chesterfield

COPYRIGHT

DISCLAIMER

The information provided in this book is for general informational purposes only. All content in this book reflects the author's views and is based on their research, knowledge, and experiences. The author and publisher make no representations or warranties of any kind concerning the completeness, accuracy, reliability, suitability, or availability of the information contained herein.

This book is not intended to be a substitute for professional advice, diagnosis, or treatment. Readers should seek professional advice for any specific concerns or conditions. The author and publisher disclaim any liability or responsibility for any direct, indirect, incidental, or consequential loss or damage arising from the use of the information contained in this book.

Contents

Chapter 1: Getting Started with Python

Welcome to the first step of your programming adventure! In this chapter, we'll introduce you to Python, set up everything you need to start coding, guide you through writing your very first Python program, and help you understand the basic building blocks of Python syntax and semantics. Let's dive in!

1.1 Introduction to Python

What is Python?

Python is a popular, high-level programming language known for its simplicity and readability. It's used by beginners and professionals alike to create websites, analyze data, build games, and even control robots! Python's easy-to-understand syntax makes it an excellent choice for those new to programming.

Why Learn Python?

- **Easy to Read and Write**: Python's syntax is clear and straightforward, making it easier to learn compared to other programming languages.

- **Versatile**: Whether you're interested in web development, data science, artificial intelligence, or game development, Python has tools and libraries to support your projects.

- **Large Community**: Python has a vast and active community, meaning plenty of resources, tutorials, and support are available.

- **Career Opportunities**: Python skills are in high demand across various industries, opening doors to numerous career paths.

Real-World Applications of Python

- **Web Development**: Building websites and web applications using frameworks like Django and Flask.

- **Data Science**: Analyzing and visualizing data with libraries like Pandas and Matplotlib.

- **Artificial Intelligence**: Creating intelligent systems with TensorFlow and Scikit-Learn.

- **Game Development**: Developing games using Pygame.

- **Automation**: Automating repetitive tasks to save time and increase productivity.

Fun Fact

Did you know that Python is named after the British comedy group "Monty Python"? The creator of Python, Guido van Rossum, wanted a name that was short, unique, and slightly mysterious!

1.2 Setting Up Your Environment

Before you start writing Python code, you need to set up your development environment. This involves installing Python on your computer and choosing an editor where you'll write your code.

Installing Python

1. **Download Python**:

   - Visit the official Python website.

   - Click on the latest version of Python (e.g., Python 3.x.x).

   - The website should automatically detect your operating system (Windows, macOS, or Linux) and provide the appropriate download link.

2. **Install Python**:

   - Run the downloaded installer.

   - **Important**: During installation, make sure to check the box that says **"Add Python to PATH"**. This allows you to run Python from the command line.

   - Follow the on-screen instructions to complete the installation.

3. **Verify the Installation**:

   - Open your terminal or command prompt.

   - Type python --version and press Enter.

- You should see the version of Python you installed (e.g., Python 3.10.4).

Choosing an Integrated Development Environment (IDE)

An IDE is a software application that provides tools to help you write and test your code efficiently. Here are some beginner-friendly IDEs:

1. **IDLE**:

   - Comes bundled with Python.

   - Simple interface suitable for beginners.

   - **How to Open**:

     - On Windows: Search for "IDLE" in the Start menu.

     - On macOS/Linux: Open your terminal and type idle3.

2. **Visual Studio Code (VS Code)**:

   - A free, powerful code editor with many extensions.

   - Supports syntax highlighting, debugging, and more.

   - **Installation**:

     - Download from Visual Studio Code.

     - After installation, you can add the Python extension for enhanced features.

3. **PyCharm**:

   - A feature-rich IDE specifically for Python development.

   - Available in both free (Community) and paid (Professional) versions.

   - **Installation**:

     - Download from PyCharm.

*For beginners, **Visual Studio Code** is highly recommended due to its user-friendly interface and extensive support through extensions.*

Setting Up Your IDE

Let's set up Visual Studio Code for Python development:

1. **Install Visual Studio Code**:

   - Download and install from the official website.

2. **Install the Python Extension**:

   - Open VS Code.

   - Click on the Extensions icon on the left sidebar (it looks like four squares).

   - Search for "Python" and install the extension provided by Microsoft.

3. **Configure Python Interpreter**:

- Press Ctrl + Shift + P (Windows/Linux) or Cmd + Shift + P (macOS) to open the command palette.
- Type Python: Select Interpreter and press Enter.
- Choose the Python version you installed earlier.

4. **Verify the Setup**:
   - Create a new file by clicking on File > New File.
   - Save the file with a .py extension, e.g., test.py.
   - Write a simple Python command, such as print("Hello, Python!").
   - Run the code by right-clicking inside the editor and selecting Run Python File in Terminal.

1.3 Writing Your First Python Program

Now that your environment is set up, it's time to write your first Python program! We'll create a simple program that greets you.

Step-by-Step Guide

1. **Open Your IDE**:

- Launch Visual Studio Code or your chosen IDE.

2. **Create a New File**:

   - Click on File > New File.

   - Save the file as hello.py by clicking File > Save As and entering the name.

3. **Write the Code**:

   - In the hello.py file, type the following code:

python

```
print("Hello, World!")
```

4. **Save the File**:

   - Press Ctrl + S (Windows/Linux) or Cmd + S (macOS) to save your changes.

5. **Run the Program**:

   - **Using the Terminal**:

     - Open the terminal in your IDE (usually found at the bottom).

     - Navigate to the directory where you saved hello.py using the cd command.

bash

cd path/to/your/file

- Type python hello.py and press Enter.

    o **Using the IDE's Built-In Features**:

    - Right-click inside the editor and select Run Python File in Terminal.

6. **See the Output**:

Hello, World!

Congratulations!

You've just written and executed your first Python program! This simple program uses the print() function to display the message "Hello, World!" on the screen.

Exploring Further

Try modifying your hello.py file to display different messages:

- **Example 1**:

python

print("Welcome to Python Programming!")

- **Example 2**:

python

```
print("Python is fun!")
```

Run the program each time to see how the output changes based on your code.

1.4 Understanding Syntax and Semantics

Before you dive deeper into Python programming, it's essential to understand the basic concepts of syntax and semantics. These terms might sound complicated, but don't worry—they're just fancy ways of talking about how code is written and what it means.

What is Syntax?

Syntax refers to the set of rules that define the structure of code. It's like the grammar of a programming language. If your code doesn't follow the correct syntax, Python won't understand it and will throw an error.

Key Points:

- **Indentation**: Python uses indentation (spaces or tabs) to define blocks of code.

- **Case Sensitivity**: Python distinguishes between uppercase and lowercase letters.

- **Proper Use of Symbols**: Correct use of parentheses, colons, commas, etc.

Example of Correct Syntax:

python

```
if 5 > 2:
    print("Five is greater than two!")
```

Example of Syntax Error:

python

```
if 5 > 2
    print("Five is greater than two!")
```

Error: Missing colon (:) after the if statement.

What is Semantics?

Semantics deals with the meaning of the code. While syntax is about how you write the code, semantics is about what the code does. Even if your code has correct syntax, it might not do what you intended if the semantics are wrong.

Key Points:

- **Logical Flow**: Ensuring your code follows a logical sequence to achieve the desired outcome.

- **Correct Operations**: Using the right operators and functions to perform tasks.

- **Meaningful Variables**: Choosing variable names that represent their purpose.

Example of Correct Semantics:

python

```python
x = 10
y = 5
print(x + y)  # This will output 15
```

Example of Semantic Error:

python

```python
# Intended to calculate the area of a rectangle
length = 5
width = 3
area = length + width  # Should be length * width
print(area)
```

Error: Using the addition operator (+) instead of multiplication (*) to calculate the area.

Combining Syntax and Semantics

Writing good code requires both correct syntax and clear semantics. Let's look at an example that combines both:

python

```python
def greet(name):
```

```python
    print(f"Hello, {name}!")
```

```python
greet("Alice")
```

- **Syntax**:
  - Correct use of def to define a function.
  - Proper indentation for the function body.
  - Correct placement of parentheses and quotes.
- **Semantics**:
  - The function greet takes a parameter name and prints a greeting.
  - When greet("Alice") is called, it outputs "Hello, Alice!".

Common Syntax and Semantic Errors

Syntax Error Example:

python

```python
print("Hello, World!"
```

Error: Missing closing parenthesis.

Solution:

python

```python
print("Hello, World!")
```

Semantic Error Example:

python

```
# Intended to subtract y from x
x = 10
y = 5
result = x + y  # Should be x - y
print(result)
```

Error. Using addition instead of subtraction.

Solution:

python

```
result = x - y
print(result)  # Outputs 5
```

Tips for Avoiding Syntax and Semantic Errors

1. **Read Error Messages Carefully:**
   - Python provides error messages that can help you identify and fix issues.

2. **Practice Proper Indentation:**
   - Consistently use spaces or tabs for indentation. Python typically uses 4 spaces per indentation level.

3. **Use Meaningful Variable Names:**

- Choose names that reflect the purpose of the variable, making your code easier to understand.

4. **Test Your Code Frequently**:
   - Run your code after writing small sections to catch errors early.

5. **Review and Refactor**:
   - Regularly review your code to improve its structure and readability.

Exercise: Fix the Errors

Below are some code snippets with errors. Identify and fix both syntax and semantic errors.

1. **Snippet 1**:

python

```
if 3 < 5
    print("Three is less than five")
```

Error: Missing colon after the if statement.

Fixed Code:

python

```
if 3 < 5:
    print("Three is less than five")
```

2. **Snippet 2**:

python

```python
def add_numbers(a, b)
    return a + b

result = add_numbers(10, 5)
print(result)
```

Error: Missing colon after the function definition.

Fixed Code:

python

```python
def add_numbers(a, b):
    return a + b

result = add_numbers(10, 5)
print(result)  # Outputs 15
```

3. **Snippet 3**:

python

```python
age = "10"
if age > 5:
    print("Age is greater than 5")
```

Error: Comparing a string with an integer.

Fixed Code:

python

```python
age = 10  # Changed to integer
if age > 5:
    print("Age is greater than 5")  # Outputs "Age is greater than 5"
```

4. **Snippet 4**:

python

```python
total = 50
tax = 0.07
final_amount = total + tax
print(final_amount)
```

Error: Semantic error—adding tax rate directly instead of calculating tax amount.

Fixed Code:

python

```python
total = 50
tax_rate = 0.07
tax_amount = total * tax_rate
```

```
final_amount = total + tax_amount

print(final_amount)  # Outputs 53.5
```

In this chapter, you've been introduced to Python and learned why it's an excellent language for beginners. You've set up your development environment, written your first Python program, and gained a basic understanding of Python's syntax and semantics. Understanding these foundational concepts is crucial as you continue your programming journey. In the next chapter, we'll explore more basic programming concepts, including variables, data types, and control structures. Keep practicing, and happy coding!

Chapter 2: Basic Programming Concepts

Welcome to **Chapter 2: Basic Programming Concepts**! Now that you've written your first Python program and have a glimpse of what Python can do, it's time to dive deeper into the foundational elements of programming. In this chapter, we'll explore variables and data types, operators and expressions, control structures like if statements and loops, and the power of functions and modules. These concepts are the building blocks that will enable you to create more complex and exciting programs. Let's get started!

2.1 Variables and Data Types

What are Variables?

Variables are like containers that hold information. Imagine them as labeled boxes where you can store different items (data) and retrieve them when needed. In programming, variables allow you to store, modify, and use data throughout your programs.

Example:

python

```python
# Storing a message in a variable
greeting = "Hello, Python!"


# Storing a number in a variable
age = 10


# Printing the variables
print(greeting)  # Outputs: Hello, Python!
print(age)       # Outputs: 10
```

Data Types

Data types specify the kind of data that can be stored in a variable. Python has several built-in data types that you'll frequently use:

1. **Integers (int)**: Whole numbers without a decimal point.

   o *Example*: 5, -3, 42

2. **Floats (float)**: Numbers with a decimal point.

   o *Example*: 3.14, -0.001, 2.718

3. **Strings (str)**: Sequences of characters enclosed in quotes.

   o *Example*: "Hello, World!", 'Python'

4. **Booleans (bool)**: Represents True or False values.

     ○ *Example*: True, False

5. **Lists (list)**: Ordered collections of items.

     ○ *Example*: [1, 2, 3], ["apple", "banana", "cherry"]

6. **Tuples (tuple)**: Ordered, immutable collections of items.

     ○ *Example*: (10, 20), ("red", "green", "blue")

7. **Dictionaries (dict)**: Unordered collections of key-value pairs.

     ○ *Example*: {"name": "Alice", "age": 10}

Declaring and Using Variables

Rules for Naming Variables:

- **Start with a Letter or Underscore**: Variable names must begin with a letter (a-z, A-Z) or an underscore (_).

- **No Spaces**: Use underscores (_) to separate words (e.g., my_age).

- **Case Sensitive**: Age and age are considered different variables.

- **Avoid Reserved Words**: Don't use Python's reserved keywords (like if, for, while, etc.) as variable names.

Examples:

python

```python
# Valid variable names
name = "Bob"
user_age = 12
_temperature = 98.6


# Invalid variable names
2nd_place = "Alice"     # Starts with a number
first name = "Charlie"  # Contains a space
class = "Mathematics"   # 'class' is a reserved keyword
```

Changing Variable Values

Variables can be updated or reassigned to hold new data.

Example:

python

```python
score = 50
print(score)  # Outputs: 50


# Updating the score
score = 75
print(score)  # Outputs: 75
```

Type Casting

Sometimes, you may need to convert one data type to another. This is called type casting.

Examples:

python

```python
# Converting integer to string
age = 10
age_str = str(age)
print("I am " + age_str + " years old.")  # Outputs: I am 10 years old.


# Converting string to integer
height_str = "150"
height = int(height_str)
print(height + 20)  # Outputs: 170


# Converting integer to float
count = 5
count_float = float(count)
print(count_float)  # Outputs: 5.0
```

Exercise: Variable Practice

1. **Create Variables**:

- Create a variable named favorite_color and assign your favorite color to it.
- Create a variable named num_candies and assign the number of candies you have.

2. **Print Variables**:

   - Print both variables to see their values.

3. **Update Variables**:

   - Change the value of num_candies to reflect eating some candies.
   - Print the updated num_candies.

Example Solution:

python

```
# Creating variables
favorite_color = "Blue"
num_candies = 20


# Printing variables
print("Favorite Color:", favorite_color)  # Outputs:
Favorite Color: Blue

print("Number of Candies:", num_candies) # Outputs:
Number of Candies: 20
```

```
# Updating variables

num_candies = 15

print("Updated Number of Candies:", num_candies)  #
Outputs: Updated Number of Candies: 15
```

2.2 Operators and Expressions

Operators are symbols that perform operations on variables and values. Expressions are combinations of variables, values, and operators that Python can evaluate to produce a result.

Types of Operators

1. **Arithmetic Operators**: Perform mathematical operations.

2. **Comparison Operators**: Compare values and return boolean results.

3. **Logical Operators**: Combine boolean expressions.

4. **Assignment Operators**: Assign values to variables.

5. **Logical Operators**: Combine multiple conditions.

2.2.1 Arithmetic Operators

Arithmetic operators allow you to perform basic mathematical operations.

Operator	Name	Example	Description
+	Addition	5 + 3	Adds two numbers
-	Subtraction	10 - 4	Subtracts the second number from the first
*	Multiplication	7 * 2	Multiplies two numbers
/	Division	8 / 2	Divides the first number by the second
%	Modulus	9 % 4	Returns the remainder of division
**	Exponentiation	2 ** 3	Raises the first number to the power of the second
//	Floor Division	7 // 2	Divides and returns the integer part

Examples:

python

Addition

```python
sum = 5 + 3
print("5 + 3 =", sum)  # Outputs: 5 + 3 = 8


# Subtraction
difference = 10 - 4
print("10 - 4 =", difference)  # Outputs: 10 - 4 = 6


# Multiplication
product = 7 * 2
print("7 * 2 =", product)  # Outputs: 7 * 2 = 14


# Division
quotient = 8 / 2
print("8 / 2 =", quotient)  # Outputs: 8 / 2 = 4.0


# Modulus
remainder = 9 % 4
print("9 % 4 =", remainder)  # Outputs: 9 % 4 = 1


# Exponentiation
power = 2 ** 3
print("2 ** 3 =", power)  # Outputs: 2 ** 3 = 8
```

```
# Floor Division

floor_div = 7 // 2

print("7 // 2 =", floor_div)  # Outputs: 7 // 2 = 3
```

2.2.2 Comparison Operators

Comparison operators compare two values and return a boolean result (True or False).

Operator	Name	Example	Description
==	Equal to	5 == 5	Returns True if both values are equal
!=	Not equal to	5 != 3	Returns True if values are not equal
>	Greater than	7 > 4	Returns True if the left value is greater
<	Less than	3 < 6	Returns True if the left value is less
>=	Greater than or equal to	5 >= 5	Returns True if the left value is greater or equal
<=	Less than or equal to	2 <= 3	Returns True if the left value is less or equal

Examples:

python

```python
# Equal to
print(5 == 5)  # Outputs: True
print(5 == 3)  # Outputs: False

# Not equal to
print(5 != 3)  # Outputs: True
print(5 != 5)  # Outputs: False

# Greater than
print(7 > 4)   # Outputs: True
print(3 > 5)   # Outputs: False

# Less than
print(3 < 6)   # Outputs: True
print(6 < 2)   # Outputs: False

# Greater than or equal to
print(5 >= 5)  # Outputs: True
print(4 >= 5)  # Outputs: False

# Less than or equal to
```

```python
print(2 <= 3)  # Outputs: True

print(5 <= 3)  # Outputs: False
```

2.2.3 Logical Operators

Logical operators allow you to combine multiple boolean expressions.

Operator	Name	Example	Description
and	Logical AND	True and False	Returns True if both expressions are True
or	Logical OR	True or False	Returns True if at least one expression is True
not	Logical NOT	not True	Inverts the boolean value

Examples:

python

```python
# Logical AND
print(True and True)   # Outputs: True
print(True and False)  # Outputs: False


# Logical OR
print(True or False)   # Outputs: True
print(False or False)  # Outputs: False
```

```
# Logical NOT
print(not True)        # Outputs: False
print(not False)       # Outputs: True


# Combining Operators
x = 5
y = 10


print(x > 2 and y < 15)  # Outputs: True
print(x == 5 or y == 5)  # Outputs: True
print(not (x > y))       # Outputs: True
```

2.2.4 Assignment Operators

Assignment operators are used to assign values to variables.

Operator	Name	Example	Description
=	Assign	x = 5	Assigns the value on the right to the variable on the left
+=	Add and Assign	x += 3	Adds the right value to the left variable and assigns the result to the left variable

Operator	Name	Example	Description
-=	Subtract and Assign	x -= 2	Subtracts the right value from the left variable and assigns the result to the left variable
*=	Multiply and Assign	x *= 4	Multiplies the left variable by the right value and assigns the result to the left variable
/=	Divide and Assign	x /= 2	Divides the left variable by the right value and assigns the result to the left variable

Examples:

python

```
# Assign
x = 5
print(x)  # Outputs: 5


# Add and Assign
x += 3  # Equivalent to x = x + 3
print(x)  # Outputs: 8
```

```python
# Subtract and Assign
x -= 2  # Equivalent to x = x - 2
print(x)  # Outputs: 6


# Multiply and Assign
x *= 4  # Equivalent to x = x * 4
print(x)  # Outputs: 24


# Divide and Assign
x /= 2  # Equivalent to x = x / 2
print(x)  # Outputs: 12.0
```

2.2.5 Operator Precedence

Operator precedence determines the order in which operations are performed in an expression. Operations with higher precedence are performed before those with lower precedence.

Precedence Order (from highest to lowest):

1. **Parentheses ()**
2. **Exponentiation ****
3. **Unary + and -**
4. **Multiplication *, Division /, Floor Division //, Modulus %**

5. **Addition +, Subtraction -**

6. **Comparison Operators**

7. **Logical NOT not**

8. **Logical AND and**

9. **Logical OR or**

Example:

python

```
result = 3 + 4 * 2  # Multiplication has higher precedence
print(result)  # Outputs: 11


# Using parentheses to change precedence
result = (3 + 4) * 2
print(result)  # Outputs: 14


# Combining different operators
result = 2 + 3 * 4 ** 2
# 4 ** 2 = 16
# 3 * 16 = 48
# 2 + 48 = 50
print(result)  # Outputs: 50
```

Exercise: Operator Practice

1. **Calculate the Area of a Rectangle**:

   o Create variables length and width.

   o Calculate the area using multiplication.

   o Print the result.

2. **Compare Two Numbers**:

   o Create two variables num1 and num2.

   o Use comparison operators to check which number is greater.

   o Print the result.

3. **Use Logical Operators**:

   o Create two boolean variables is_raining and has_umbrella.

   o Determine if you can go outside without getting wet using logical operators.

   o Print the result.

Example Solution:

python

```
# 1. Calculate the Area of a Rectangle
length = 5
width = 3
area = length * width
```

```
print("Area of the rectangle:", area)  # Outputs: Area
of the rectangle: 15


# 2. Compare Two Numbers

num1 = 10

num2 = 7

print("Is num1 greater than num2?", num1 > num2)  #
Outputs: Is num1 greater than num2? True


# 3. Use Logical Operators

is_raining = True

has_umbrella = False

can_go_outside = not is_raining or has_umbrella

print("Can you go outside without getting wet?",
can_go_outside)  # Outputs: Can you go outside
without getting wet? False
```

2.3 Control Structures: If Statements and Loops

Control structures dictate the flow of your program, allowing you to make decisions and repeat actions. In this section, we'll explore **if statements** for decision-making and **loops** for repeating tasks.

2.3.1 If Statements

If statements allow your program to execute certain blocks of code based on specific conditions.

Basic If Statement

python

```
age = 10

if age >= 18:
    print("You are an adult.")
```

Output: (Nothing, because age is not greater than or equal to 18.)

If-Else Statement

python

```
age = 10

if age >= 18:
    print("You are an adult.")
else:
    print("You are a child.")
```

Output:

css

You are a child.

If-Elif-Else Statement

python

score = 85

```python
if score >= 90:
    print("Grade: A")
elif score >= 80:
    print("Grade: B")
elif score >= 70:
    print("Grade: C")
else:
    print("Grade: F")
```

Output:

makefile

Grade: B

2.3.2 Nested If Statements

You can place if statements inside other if statements to check multiple conditions.

Example:

python

```python
temperature = 25

if temperature > 30:
    print("It's a hot day.")
    if temperature > 35:
        print("Stay hydrated!")
else:
    print("The weather is pleasant.")
```

Output:

csharp

```
The weather is pleasant.
```

2.3.3 Logical Operators in If Statements

Combine multiple conditions using logical operators.

Example:

python

```python
age = 16
has_permission = True

if age >= 18 and has_permission:
    print("You can enter the club.")
elif age >= 16 and has_permission:
    print("You can enter with parental consent.")
else:
    print("You cannot enter the club.")
```

Output:

csharp

You can enter with parental consent.

2.3.4 Loops

Loops allow you to execute a block of code multiple times. Python has two main types of loops: **for loops** and **while loops**.

For Loops

For loops are used to iterate over a sequence (like a list, tuple, or string) or a range of numbers.

Example: Iterating Over a List

python

```python
fruits = ["apple", "banana", "cherry"]

for fruit in fruits:
    print(fruit)
```
Output:

apple

banana

cherry

Example: Using Range

python

```python
for i in range(5):
    print(i)
```
Output:

0

1

2

3

4

Using range(start, stop, step)

python

```python
for i in range(2, 10, 2):
    print(i)
```

Output:

```
2
4
6
8
```

While Loops

While loops continue to execute as long as a condition is True.

Example:

python

```python
count = 0

while count < 5:
    print(count)
    count += 1
```

Output:

0

1

2

3

4

Infinite Loop Warning

Be cautious to ensure that the condition in a while loop will eventually become False. Otherwise, you'll create an infinite loop that never stops.

python

```python
# This will create an infinite loop
count = 0

while count < 5:
    print(count)
    # Missing count increment
```

2.3.5 Break and Continue Statements

Break and **continue** statements provide additional control within loops.

Break Statement

The break statement exits the loop immediately.

Example:

python

```
for i in range(10):
    if i == 5:
        break
    print(i)
```

Output:

```
0
1
2
3
4
```

Continue Statement

The continue statement skips the current iteration and moves to the next one.

Example:

python

```
for i in range(5):
```

```python
    if i == 2:
        continue
    print(i)
```

Output:

```
0
1
3
4
```

2.3.6 Nested Loops

Loops can be placed inside other loops, allowing for more complex iterations.

Example: Multiplication Table

python

```python
for i in range(1, 4):
    for j in range(1, 4):
        product = i * j
        print(f"{i} * {j} = {product}")
    print("---")
```

Output:

yaml

1 * 1 = 1

1 * 2 = 2

1 * 3 = 3

---

2 * 1 = 2

2 * 2 = 4

2 * 3 = 6

---

3 * 1 = 3

3 * 2 = 6

3 * 3 = 9

Exercise: Control Structures Practice

1. **Even or Odd Checker**:
   - Ask the user to input a number.
   - Use an if-else statement to determine if the number is even or odd.
   - Print the result.

2. **Countdown Timer**:
   - Use a while loop to count down from 10 to 1.
   - Print each number.

o   After reaching 1, print "Liftoff!"

3. **Number List Filter**:

  o   Create a list of numbers from 1 to 10.

  o   Use a for loop to print only the numbers that are divisible by 3.

Example Solution:

python

```python
# 1. Even or Odd Checker
number = int(input("Enter a number: "))

if number % 2 == 0:
    print(number, "is even.")
else:
    print(number, "is odd.")

# 2. Countdown Timer
count = 10

while count > 0:
    print(count)
    count -= 1
```

```
print("Liftoff!")


# 3. Number List Filter
numbers = list(range(1, 11))


print("Numbers divisible by 3:")
for num in numbers:
    if num % 3 == 0:
        print(num)
```

Sample Interaction:

csharp

Enter a number: 7

7 is odd.

10

9

8

7

6

5

4

3

2

1

Liftoff!

Numbers divisible by 3:

3

6

9

2.4 Functions and Modules

Functions and modules help organize your code, making it reusable and easier to manage. Functions allow you to encapsulate code into blocks that perform specific tasks, while modules let you group related functions together.

2.4.1 Functions

A **function** is a block of reusable code that performs a specific task. Functions help make your code more organized and avoid repetition.

Defining a Function

Use the def keyword to define a function.

Example: Greeting Function

python

```python
def greet():
    print("Hello, there!")
```

Calling a Function

python

```python
greet()  # Outputs: Hello, there!
greet()  # Outputs: Hello, there!
```

Functions with Parameters

Parameters allow you to pass information to functions.

Example: Personalized Greeting

python

```python
def greet(name):
    print(f"Hello, {name}!")
```

```python
greet("Alice")  # Outputs: Hello, Alice!
greet("Bob")    # Outputs: Hello, Bob!
```

Functions with Return Values

Functions can return values using the return statement.

Example: Addition Function

python

```python
def add(a, b):
    return a + b

result = add(5, 3)
print("5 + 3 =", result)  # Outputs: 5 + 3 = 8
```

Default Parameters

You can assign default values to parameters, which are used if no argument is provided.

Example: Greeting with Default Name

python

```python
def greet(name="Friend"):
    print(f"Hello, {name}!")

greet("Alice")  # Outputs: Hello, Alice!
greet()         # Outputs: Hello, Friend!
```

Keyword Arguments

When calling functions, you can specify arguments by their parameter names.

Example:

python

```python
def describe_pet(animal_type, pet_name):
    print(f"\nI have a {animal_type}.")
    print(f"My {animal_type}'s name is {pet_name}.")


describe_pet(animal_type="hamster",
pet_name="Harry")
```

Output:

css

I have a hamster.

My hamster's name is Harry.

2.4.2 Return Statement

The return statement sends back a result from a function to the caller.

Example: Calculate Square

python

```python
def square(number):
    return number * number


result = square(4)
```

```python
print("Square of 4 is", result)  # Outputs: Square of 4
is 16
```

2.4.3 Scope of Variables

Variables defined inside a function are **local** to that function and cannot be accessed outside.

Example:

python

```python
def my_function():

    local_var = 10

    print("Inside function:", local_var)


my_function()        # Outputs: Inside function: 10

print(local_var)      # Raises an error: NameError:
name 'local_var' is not defined
```

2.4.4 Lambda Functions

Lambda functions are small, anonymous functions defined with the lambda keyword. They're useful for short, simple operations.

Example: Lambda Function for Addition

python

```python
add = lambda a, b: a + b

print(add(3, 5))  # Outputs: 8
```

2.4.5 Modules

A **module** is a file containing Python code (functions, variables, classes) that can be imported and used in other programs. Modules help organize code and promote reusability.

Creating a Module

1. **Create a Python File**: For example, create a file named math_utils.py.

2. **Define Functions in the Module**:

python

```
# math_utils.py


def add(a, b):
    return a + b


def subtract(a, b):
    return a - b
```

Importing a Module

You can import the entire module or specific functions from it.

Example: Importing the Entire Module

python

```
import math_utils
```

```
result = math_utils.add(10, 5)
```

```
print("10 + 5 =", result)  # Outputs: 10 + 5 = 15
```

Example: Importing Specific Functions

python

```
from math_utils import subtract
```

```
result = subtract(10, 5)
```

```
print("10 - 5 =", result)  # Outputs: 10 - 5 = 5
```

Example: Importing with an Alias

python

```
import math_utils as mu
```

```
result = mu.add(7, 3)
```

```
print("7 + 3 =", result)  # Outputs: 7 + 3 = 10
```

Using Built-in Modules

Python comes with a variety of built-in modules that provide additional functionality.

Example: Using the math Module

```python
import math

# Using the sqrt function to calculate the square root
print(math.sqrt(16))  # Outputs: 4.0

# Using the pi constant
print(math.pi)      # Outputs: 3.141592653589793
```

2.4.6 The import Statement

The import statement is used to include modules in your program.

Syntax:

```python
import module_name
```

Example:

```python
import random

print(random.randint(1, 10))  # Outputs a random
integer between 1 and 10
```

Exercise: Functions and Modules Practice

1. **Create a Greeting Function**:

   - Define a function welcome() that prints "Welcome to Python Programming!"

   - Call the function.

2. **Calculator Module**:

   - Create a module named calculator.py.

   - In calculator.py, define functions multiply(a, b) and divide(a, b).

   - In your main program, import the calculator module.

   - Use the imported functions to perform multiplication and division, and print the results.

3. **Using Built-in Modules**:

   - Import the random module.

   - Generate and print a random number between 1 and 100.

Example Solution:

python

```python
# 1. Create a Greeting Function
def welcome():
    print("Welcome to Python Programming!")
```

```python
welcome()  # Outputs: Welcome to Python Programming!


# 2. Calculator Module

# Create a file named calculator.py with the following content:
"""

# calculator.py


def multiply(a, b):
    return a * b


def divide(a, b):
    if b != 0:
        return a / b
    else:
        return "Cannot divide by zero."
"""


# In your main program:
import calculator
```

```
product = calculator.multiply(6, 7)
print("6 * 7 =", product)  # Outputs: 6 * 7 = 42


quotient = calculator.divide(10, 2)
print("10 / 2 =", quotient)  # Outputs: 10 / 2 = 5.0


quotient = calculator.divide(10, 0)
print("10 / 0 =", quotient)  # Outputs: 10 / 0 = Cannot
divide by zero.


# 3. Using Built-in Modules
import random


random_number = random.randint(1, 100)
print("Random number between 1 and 100:",
random_number)  # Outputs a random number, e.g.,
57
```

Note: To create a module like calculator.py, you need to create a new file in the same directory as your main program and paste the function definitions there.

Chapter 3: Working with Data

Welcome to **Chapter 3: Working with Data**! In this chapter, we'll explore how Python can help you manage and analyze data. Whether you're keeping track of your favorite games, managing a list of friends, or analyzing sports statistics, understanding how to work with data is essential. We'll introduce you to the basics of data science, delve into Python's fundamental data structures—lists, tuples, and dictionaries—and learn how to read and write files. Finally, we'll take a peek into **Pandas**, a powerful library for data manipulation. Let's get started!

3.1 Introduction to Data Science

What is Data Science?

Data Science is a field that involves collecting, analyzing, and interpreting large amounts of data to discover patterns, make decisions, and solve problems. Imagine being able to predict the next big game trend, understand your friends' favorite activities, or even analyze your school's sports performance—all through data!

Why is Data Science Important?

- **Informed Decision Making**: Helps in making decisions based on data rather than guesswork.

- **Identifying Trends**: Uncovers patterns and trends that aren't immediately obvious.

- **Problem Solving**: Provides solutions to real-world problems using data insights.

- **Innovation**: Drives advancements in technology, healthcare, finance, and more.

Real-World Applications of Data Science

- **Sports Analytics**: Analyzing player performance and team strategies.

- **Healthcare**: Predicting disease outbreaks and improving patient care.

- **Finance**: Detecting fraudulent transactions and managing investments.

- **Entertainment**: Recommending movies or songs based on your preferences.

- **Education**: Tracking student performance and improving learning methods.

Fun Fact

Did you know that data science is used to recommend the next episode you should watch on streaming platforms like Netflix? By analyzing your viewing history, data science helps tailor your entertainment experience!

3.2 Lists, Tuples, and Dictionaries

Python offers several data structures to store and organize data. The most common ones are **lists**, **tuples**, and **dictionaries**. Understanding these will help you manage data effectively in your programs.

3.2.1 Lists

Lists are ordered, mutable (changeable) collections of items. They are perfect for storing sequences of data, such as a list of your favorite games or the names of your friends.

Creating a List

python

```
# Creating a list of favorite fruits

fruits = ["apple", "banana", "cherry"]

print(fruits)  # Outputs: ['apple', 'banana', 'cherry']
```

Accessing List Items

You can access items in a list by their index (position). Python uses **zero-based indexing**, meaning the first item is at index 0.

python

```
# Accessing items by index

print(fruits[0])  # Outputs: apple
```

```python
print(fruits[2])  # Outputs: cherry
```

Modifying List Items

Since lists are mutable, you can change their contents.

python

```python
# Changing the second item
fruits[1] = "blueberry"
print(fruits)  # Outputs: ['apple', 'blueberry', 'cherry']
```

Adding Items to a List

python

```python
# Adding an item to the end of the list
fruits.append("date")
print(fruits)  # Outputs: ['apple', 'blueberry', 'cherry', 'date']
```

Removing Items from a List

python

```python
# Removing an item by value
fruits.remove("blueberry")
print(fruits)  # Outputs: ['apple', 'cherry', 'date']
```

```python
# Removing an item by index
removed_fruit = fruits.pop(1)
print(removed_fruit)  # Outputs: cherry
print(fruits)         # Outputs: ['apple', 'date']
```

3.2.2 Tuples

Tuples are ordered, immutable (unchangeable) collections of items. They are useful for storing data that shouldn't be modified, such as the coordinates of a point or the days of the week.

Creating a Tuple

python

```python
# Creating a tuple of coordinates
coordinates = (10.0, 20.0)
print(coordinates)  # Outputs: (10.0, 20.0)
```

Accessing Tuple Items

Similar to lists, you can access tuple items by their index.

python

```python
# Accessing items by index
print(coordinates[0])  # Outputs: 10.0
print(coordinates[1])  # Outputs: 20.0
```

Attempting to Modify a Tuple

python

```
# Trying to change a tuple item (This will raise an error)
coordinates[0] = 15.0  # TypeError: 'tuple' object does not support item assignment
```

3.2.3 Dictionaries

Dictionaries are unordered collections of key-value pairs. They are perfect for storing related data, like a person's name and age or a student's grades.

Creating a Dictionary

python

```
# Creating a dictionary of a person
person = {
    "name": "Alice",
    "age": 10,
    "favorite_game": "Minecraft"
}
print(person)  # Outputs: {'name': 'Alice', 'age': 10, 'favorite_game': 'Minecraft'}
```

Accessing Dictionary Values

You access values in a dictionary by their keys.

```python
python
```

```python
# Accessing values by key
print(person["name"])        # Outputs: Alice
print(person["favorite_game"]) # Outputs: Minecraft
```

Modifying Dictionary Values

```python
python
```

```python
# Changing the age
person["age"] = 11
print(person)  # Outputs: {'name': 'Alice', 'age': 11, 'favorite_game': 'Minecraft'}
```

Adding and Removing Key-Value Pairs

```python
python
```

```python
# Adding a new key-value pair
person["hobby"] = "drawing"
print(person)  # Outputs: {'name': 'Alice', 'age': 11, 'favorite_game': 'Minecraft', 'hobby': 'drawing'}


# Removing a key-value pair
del person["favorite_game"]
```

```
print(person)  # Outputs: {'name': 'Alice', 'age': 11,
'hobby': 'drawing'}
```

3.2.4 Comparing Lists, Tuples, and Dictionaries

Feature	List	Tuple	Dictionary
Ordered	Yes	Yes	No
Mutable	Yes	No	Yes
Indexing	Yes	Yes	No (access by keys)
Duplicate Items	Allowed	Allowed	Keys must be unique
Use Cases	Storing sequences, ordered data	Storing fixed collections, constants	Storing related key-value pairs

Exercise: Working with Data Structures

1. **Create and Modify a List**:

   o Create a list named pets containing your three favorite animals.

   o Add another animal to the list.

   o Remove the second animal from the list.

   o Print the final list.

2. **Create a Tuple**:

   o Create a tuple named dimensions with three numbers representing the length, width, and height of a box.

  o Print each dimension.

3. **Create and Update a Dictionary**:

    o Create a dictionary named student with keys name, grade, and favorite_subject.

    o Update the grade.

    o Add a new key clubs with a list of clubs the student is part of.

    o Print the updated dictionary.

Example Solution:

python

```
# 1. Create and Modify a List

pets = ["dog", "cat", "rabbit"]

print("Original pets list:", pets)  # Outputs: Original pets list: ['dog', 'cat', 'rabbit']


pets.append("hamster")

print("After adding a pet:", pets)  # Outputs: After adding a pet: ['dog', 'cat', 'rabbit', 'hamster']


pets.pop(1)  # Removes 'cat'

print("After removing the second pet:", pets)  # Outputs: After removing the second pet: ['dog', 'rabbit', 'hamster']
```

```python
# 2. Create a Tuple
dimensions = (5, 10, 15)
print("Box dimensions:")
print("Length:", dimensions[0])  # Outputs: Length: 5
print("Width:", dimensions[1])   # Outputs: Width: 10
print("Height:", dimensions[2])  # Outputs: Height: 15


# 3. Create and Update a Dictionary
student = {
    "name": "Bob",
    "grade": "5th",
    "favorite_subject": "Mathematics"
}
print("Original student dictionary:", student)
# Outputs: Original student dictionary: {'name': 'Bob',
'grade': '5th', 'favorite_subject': 'Mathematics'}


student["grade"] = "6th"
student["clubs"] = ["Chess Club", "Robotics Club"]
print("Updated student dictionary:", student)
```

```
# Outputs: Updated student dictionary: {'name': 'Bob',
'grade': '6th', 'favorite_subject': 'Mathematics', 'clubs':
['Chess Club', 'Robotics Club']}
```

3.3 Reading and Writing Files

Files allow you to store data permanently on your computer. Python provides easy ways to read from and write to files, enabling you to save your data and access it later.

3.3.1 Reading Files

To read from a file, you need to open it in **read mode** ('r'), read its contents, and then close it.

Example: Reading a Text File

Assume you have a file named story.txt with the following content:

css

Once upon a time in a land far, far away, there lived a brave knight.

python


```python
# Opening and reading a file
with open("story.txt", "r") as file:
    content = file.read()
```

```
print(content)
```

Output:

css

Once upon a time in a land far, far away, there lived a brave knight.

Explanation:

- The with statement ensures the file is properly closed after its suite finishes.

- file.read() reads the entire content of the file.

3.3.2 Writing Files

To write to a file, open it in **write mode** ('w'). This will create the file if it doesn't exist or overwrite it if it does.

Example: Writing to a Text File

python

```
# Writing to a file

with open("greeting.txt", "w") as file:

    file.write("Hello, Python Learner!\n")

    file.write("Welcome to the world of programming.")
```

After running the above code, the greeting.txt file will contain:

css

Hello, Python Learner!

Welcome to the world of programming.

3.3.3 Appending to Files

To add content to the end of an existing file without overwriting it, use **append mode** ('a').

Example: Appending to a File

python

```
# Appending to a file

with open("greeting.txt", "a") as file:

    file.write("\nEnjoy your coding journey!")
```

The greeting.txt file now contains:

css

Hello, Python Learner!

Welcome to the world of programming.

Enjoy your coding journey!

3.3.4 Reading Files Line by Line

Sometimes, it's useful to read a file one line at a time, especially for large files.

Example: Reading a File Line by Line

python

```python
# Reading a file line by line
with open("story.txt", "r") as file:
    for line in file:
        print(line.strip())  # strip() removes leading/trailing whitespace
```

Output:

css

Once upon a time in a land far, far away, there lived a brave knight.

3.3.5 Handling Exceptions

When working with files, it's essential to handle potential errors, such as the file not existing.

Example: Handling File Not Found Error

python

```python
try:
    with open("nonexistent.txt", "r") as file:
        content = file.read()
        print(content)
except FileNotFoundError:
    print("Sorry, the file does not exist.")
```

Output:

Sorry, the file does not exist.

Exercise: Reading and Writing Files

1. **Create a Diary Entry**:
    - Write a program that asks the user to enter a diary entry.
    - Append the entry to a file named diary.txt.
    - Confirm to the user that the entry has been saved.

2. **Read Your Diary**:
    - Write a program that reads and prints all entries from diary.txt.

3. **Favorite Books List**:
    - Write a program that writes a list of your five favorite books to a file named books.txt.
    - Then, write another program that reads and prints the list of books.

Example Solution:

python

1. Create a Diary Entry

```python
entry = input("Enter your diary entry: ")

with open("diary.txt", "a") as file:
    file.write(entry + "\n")


print("Your diary entry has been saved.")


# 2. Read Your Diary
try:
    with open("diary.txt", "r") as file:
        print("\nYour Diary Entries:")
        for line in file:
            print(line.strip())
except FileNotFoundError:
    print("No diary entries found.")


# 3. Favorite Books List
favorite_books = [
    "Harry Potter and the Sorcerer's Stone",
    "The Hobbit",
    "Percy Jackson and the Olympians",
    "The Maze Runner",
```

```python
    "Diary of a Wimpy Kid"
]

with open("books.txt", "w") as file:
    for book in favorite_books:
        file.write(book + "\n")

print("\nYour favorite books have been saved to books.txt.")

# Reading and printing the list of books
with open("books.txt", "r") as file:
    print("\nYour Favorite Books:")
    for book in file:
        print(book.strip())
```

Sample Interaction:

mathematica

Enter your diary entry: Today I learned about Python data structures!

Your diary entry has been saved.

Your Diary Entries:

Today I learned about Python data structures!

Your favorite books have been saved to books.txt.

Your Favorite Books:

Harry Potter and the Sorcerer's Stone

The Hobbit

Percy Jackson and the Olympians

The Maze Runner

Diary of a Wimpy Kid

3.4 Basic Data Manipulation with Pandas

Pandas is a powerful Python library used for data manipulation and analysis. It provides data structures like **DataFrames** that make it easy to handle structured data. While Pandas might sound complex, we'll introduce you to the basics so you can start exploring data in no time!

3.4.1 Installing Pandas

Before using Pandas, you need to install it. You can install Pandas using **pip**, Python's package installer.

bash

```
pip install pandas
```

Note: If you're using an IDE like Visual Studio Code, you can run this command in the integrated terminal.

3.4.2 Importing Pandas

To use Pandas in your Python script, you need to import it.

python

```
import pandas as pd
```

Convention: Pandas is commonly imported with the alias pd for brevity.

3.4.3 Creating a DataFrame

A **DataFrame** is a two-dimensional table where data is organized in rows and columns, similar to a spreadsheet.

Example: Creating a DataFrame from a Dictionary

python

```
import pandas as pd


# Creating a dictionary of data
data = {
    "Name": ["Alice", "Bob", "Charlie"],
```

```
    "Age": [10, 12, 11],
    "Grade": ["5th", "6th", "5th"]
}


# Creating a DataFrame
df = pd.DataFrame(data)


print(df)
```

Output:

markdown

```
    Name  Age Grade
0   Alice  10  5th
1     Bob  12  6th
2 Charlie  11  5th
```

3.4.4 Reading a CSV File

CSV (**Comma-Separated Values**) files are commonly used to store tabular data. Pandas makes it easy to read CSV files into DataFrames.

Example: Reading a CSV File

Assume you have a CSV file named students.csv with the following content:

```
Name,Age,Grade
Alice,10,5th
Bob,12,6th
Charlie,11,5th
```

python

```python
import pandas as pd

# Reading the CSV file into a DataFrame
df = pd.read_csv("students.csv")

print(df)
```

Output:

markdown

```
      Name  Age Grade
0    Alice   10   5th
1      Bob   12   6th
2  Charlie   11   5th
```

3.4.5 Exploring Data with Pandas

Once your data is in a DataFrame, you can perform various operations to explore and analyze it.

Viewing the Data

python

```
# Display the first few rows
print(df.head())  # Shows the first 5 rows by default


# Display the last few rows
print(df.tail())  # Shows the last 5 rows by default
```

Getting Information About the DataFrame

python

```
# Get a summary of the DataFrame
print(df.info())


# Get basic statistics
print(df.describe())
```

Selecting Specific Columns

python

```
# Selecting a single column
print(df["Name"])
```

```python
# Selecting multiple columns
print(df[["Name", "Grade"]])
```

Filtering Data

python

```python
# Filtering rows where Age is greater than 10
filtered_df = df[df["Age"] > 10]
print(filtered_df)
```

Output:

markdown

```
    Name  Age Grade
1    Bob   12  6th
2 Charlie  11  5th
```

Adding New Columns

python

```python
# Adding a new column for favorite subject
df["Favorite_Subject"] = ["Math", "Science", "Art"]
print(df)
```

Output:

javascript

	Name	Age	Grade	Favorite_Subject
0	Alice	10	5th	Math
1	Bob	12	6th	Science
2	Charlie	11	5th	Art

3.4.6 Writing Data to a CSV File

After manipulating your data, you might want to save the changes to a new CSV file.

python

```
# Writing the DataFrame to a new CSV file
df.to_csv("updated_students.csv", index=False)
```

Note: The index=False parameter prevents Pandas from writing row indices to the CSV file.

Exercise: Basic Data Manipulation with Pandas

1. **Create a DataFrame**:
   - Create a dictionary with the following data:
     - Name: ["Daisy", "Ethan", "Fiona"]
     - Age: [9, 10, 11]
     - Grade: ["4th", "5th", "5th"]
   - Convert the dictionary into a Pandas DataFrame.

- o Print the DataFrame.

2. **Read and Update CSV Data**:
   - o Read the students.csv file into a DataFrame.
   - o Add a new column Favorite_Sport with values ["Soccer", "Basketball", "Baseball"].
   - o Filter the DataFrame to show only students in "5th" grade.
   - o Save the filtered data to a new CSV file named fifth_grade_students.csv.

3. **Analyze Data**:
   - o Using the updated_students.csv file created earlier, calculate the average age of the students.
   - o Print the result.

Example Solution:

python

import pandas as pd

1. Create a DataFrame

data = {

   "Name": ["Daisy", "Ethan", "Fiona"],

```python
    "Age": [9, 10, 11],
    "Grade": ["4th", "5th", "5th"]
}

df = pd.DataFrame(data)
print("Created DataFrame:")
print(df)
# Outputs:
#    Name  Age Grade
# 0  Daisy   9   4th
# 1  Ethan  10   5th
# 2  Fiona  11   5th

# 2. Read and Update CSV Data
# Reading students.csv
students_df = pd.read_csv("students.csv")

# Adding Favorite_Sport column
students_df["Favorite_Sport"] = ["Soccer", "Basketball", "Baseball"]
print("\nUpdated students DataFrame:")
print(students_df)
```

```python
# Outputs:
#     Name  Age Grade Favorite_Sport
# 0   Alice  10  5th      Soccer
# 1     Bob  12  6th    Basketball
# 2 Charlie  11  5th      Baseball


# Filtering for 5th grade students
fifth_grade_df = students_df[students_df["Grade"] ==
"5th"]
print("\nFifth Grade Students:")
print(fifth_grade_df)
# Outputs:
#     Name  Age Grade Favorite_Sport
# 0   Alice  10  5th      Soccer
# 2 Charlie  11  5th      Baseball


# Saving to a new CSV file
fifth_grade_df.to_csv("fifth_grade_students.csv",
index=False)
print("\nFifth grade students have been saved to
fifth_grade_students.csv.")


# 3. Analyze Data
```

```python
# Reading the updated_students.csv

updated_df = pd.read_csv("updated_students.csv")


# Calculating the average age

average_age = updated_df["Age"].mean()

print("\nAverage Age of Students:", average_age)  #
Outputs: Average Age of Students: 11.0
```

Note: Ensure that the CSV files (students.csv, updated_students.csv, etc.) are in the same directory as your Python script or provide the correct file paths.

Chapter 4: Creating Games with Python

Welcome to **Chapter 4: Creating Games with Python**! Now that you've grasped the fundamentals of Python and data manipulation, it's time to dive into the exciting world of game development. In this chapter, we'll introduce you to **Pygame**, a popular library for building games in Python. You'll learn how to create a simple Pong game, enhance it with graphics and sound, and add more features to make your game even more engaging. By the end of this chapter, you'll have the skills to bring your game ideas to life. Let's get started!

4.1 Introduction to Pygame

What is Pygame?

Pygame is an open-source Python library designed for creating video games. It provides functionalities for handling graphics, sound, and user input, making it easier to develop games without needing to build everything from scratch. Whether you're interested in making simple 2D games or more complex projects, Pygame offers the tools you need to get started.

Why Use Pygame?

- **Beginner-Friendly**: Pygame is accessible to those new to programming and game development.

- **Comprehensive Documentation**: Extensive resources and tutorials are available to help you learn.

- **Active Community**: A vibrant community of developers who share knowledge and support each other.

- **Versatile**: Suitable for creating a wide range of games, from simple puzzles to action-packed adventures.

Installing Pygame

Before you can start using Pygame, you need to install it. Follow these steps to get set up:

1. **Open Your Terminal or Command Prompt**:

   - **Windows**: Search for "Command Prompt" in the Start menu.

   - **macOS/Linux**: Open the Terminal application.

2. **Install Pygame Using pip**:

bash

```
pip install pygame
```

3. **Verify the Installation**:

- Open Python in your terminal by typing python or python3 and pressing Enter.

- Try importing Pygame:

```python
import pygame

print(pygame.__version__)
```

- If installed correctly, this will print the version number of Pygame.

Note: If you encounter any issues during installation, ensure that Python and pip are correctly installed and updated on your system.

Setting Up Your First Pygame Project

1. **Create a New Python File**:

   - Open your IDE (e.g., Visual Studio Code).

   - Create a new file named game.py.

2. **Initialize Pygame**:

```python
import pygame


# Initialize Pygame
pygame.init()
```

```python
# Set up the game window
screen = pygame.display.set_mode((800, 600))
pygame.display.set_caption("My First Pygame Project")

# Main game loop
running = True
while running:
    for event in pygame.event.get():
        if event.type == pygame.QUIT:
            running = False

    # Fill the screen with a color (RGB)
    screen.fill((0, 0, 0))  # Black background

    # Update the display
    pygame.display.flip()

# Quit Pygame
pygame.quit()
```

3. **Run Your Game:**

- o   Save the game.py file.

- o   Run the script using your IDE or via the terminal:

bash

python game.py

- o   A black window titled "My First Pygame Project" should appear. Close the window to end the game.

Congratulations! You've successfully set up your first Pygame project.

4.2 Building a Simple Pong Game

Let's create a classic Pong game. Pong is a two-player game where each player controls a paddle to hit a ball back and forth. The objective is to prevent the ball from passing your paddle while trying to get it past your opponent's paddle.

Step 1: Setting Up the Game Window

We've already set up the basic game window in the introduction. Let's enhance it by defining some constants and setting up the game's main elements.

Code:

python

```python
import pygame

# Initialize Pygame
pygame.init()

# Screen dimensions
SCREEN_WIDTH = 800
SCREEN_HEIGHT = 600

# Colors (RGB)
WHITE = (255, 255, 255)
BLACK = (0, 0, 0)

# Paddle properties
PADDLE_WIDTH = 10
PADDLE_HEIGHT = 100
PADDLE_SPEED = 5

# Ball properties
BALL_SIZE = 20
BALL_SPEED_X = 4
```

```python
BALL_SPEED_Y = 4


# Set up the display

screen = pygame.display.set_mode((SCREEN_WIDTH, SCREEN_HEIGHT))

pygame.display.set_caption("Pong Game")


# Define paddles and ball using pygame.Rect

left_paddle = pygame.Rect(50, SCREEN_HEIGHT//2 - PADDLE_HEIGHT//2, PADDLE_WIDTH, PADDLE_HEIGHT)

right_paddle = pygame.Rect(SCREEN_WIDTH - 50 - PADDLE_WIDTH, SCREEN_HEIGHT//2 - PADDLE_HEIGHT//2, PADDLE_WIDTH, PADDLE_HEIGHT)

ball = pygame.Rect(SCREEN_WIDTH//2 - BALL_SIZE//2, SCREEN_HEIGHT//2 - BALL_SIZE//2, BALL_SIZE, BALL_SIZE)


# Main game loop

running = True

clock = pygame.time.Clock()


while running:
```

```python
    # Handle events
    for event in pygame.event.get():
        if event.type == pygame.QUIT:
            running = False

    # Fill the screen with black
    screen.fill(BLACK)

    # Draw paddles and ball
    pygame.draw.rect(screen, WHITE, left_paddle)
    pygame.draw.rect(screen, WHITE, right_paddle)
    pygame.draw.ellipse(screen, WHITE, ball)

    # Update the display
    pygame.display.flip()

    # Cap the frame rate
    clock.tick(60)

# Quit Pygame
pygame.quit()
```
Explanation:

- **Constants**: Define screen dimensions, colors, paddle and ball properties.

- **Rect Objects**: Use pygame.Rect to represent paddles and the ball.

- **Main Loop**: Handles events, draws the game elements, and updates the display at 60 FPS.

Step 2: Adding Paddle Movement

Allow players to move their paddles up and down using keyboard inputs.

Code Enhancements:

Add the following inside the main game loop, before drawing the paddles and ball:

python

```
# Get the state of all keyboard buttons

keys = pygame.key.get_pressed()


# Move left paddle (Player 1) using 'W' and 'S' keys

if keys[pygame.K_w] and left_paddle.top > 0:

    left_paddle.y -= PADDLE_SPEED

if keys[pygame.K_s] and left_paddle.bottom <
SCREEN_HEIGHT:

    left_paddle.y += PADDLE_SPEED
```

```python
# Move right paddle (Player 2) using Up and Down
arrow keys

if keys[pygame.K_UP] and right_paddle.top > 0:

    right_paddle.y -= PADDLE_SPEED

if keys[pygame.K_DOWN] and right_paddle.bottom <
SCREEN_HEIGHT:

    right_paddle.y += PADDLE_SPEED
```

Explanation:

- **Keyboard Input**: Use pygame.key.get_pressed() to detect key presses.

- **Player Controls**:

  o **Player 1**: 'W' to move up, 'S' to move down.

  o **Player 2**: Up arrow to move up, Down arrow to move down.

- **Boundary Check**: Ensure paddles don't move off the screen.

Step 3: Adding Ball Movement and Collision

Implement ball movement and handle collisions with paddles and screen boundaries.

Code Enhancements:

Add the following before drawing the ball:

python

```
# Move the ball
ball.x += BALL_SPEED_X
ball.y += BALL_SPEED_Y


# Collision with top and bottom
if ball.top <= 0 or ball.bottom >= SCREEN_HEIGHT:
    BALL_SPEED_Y *= -1


# Collision with paddles
if ball.colliderect(left_paddle) or
ball.colliderect(right_paddle):
    BALL_SPEED_X *= -1
```

Explanation:

- **Ball Movement**: Update the ball's position by its speed.

- **Screen Collision**: Reverse vertical speed if the ball hits the top or bottom.

- **Paddle Collision**: Reverse horizontal speed if the ball collides with a paddle.

Step 4: Implementing Scoring

Keep track of player scores and display them on the screen.

Code Enhancements:

1. **Initialize Scores**:

python

```python
score_left = 0
score_right = 0
```

2. **Detect Scoring**: Add the following after handling ball movement:

python

```python
# Scoring
if ball.left <= 0:
    score_right += 1
    # Reset ball to center
    ball.center = (SCREEN_WIDTH//2,
SCREEN_HEIGHT//2)
    BALL_SPEED_X *= -1  # Change direction

if ball.right >= SCREEN_WIDTH:
    score_left += 1
    # Reset ball to center
    ball.center = (SCREEN_WIDTH//2,
SCREEN_HEIGHT//2)
    BALL_SPEED_X *= -1  # Change direction
```

3. **Display Scores**:

- o **Initialize Font**:

python

```
pygame.font.init()

font = pygame.font.SysFont(None, 36)
```

- o **Render and Blit Scores**: Add the following before updating the display:

python

```
# Render scores

score_text = font.render(f"{score_left}   {score_right}", True, WHITE)

# Position the score at the top center

screen.blit(score_text, (SCREEN_WIDTH//2 - score_text.get_width()//2, 20))
```

Explanation:

- **Scores**: Increment the appropriate player's score when the ball passes their paddle.

- **Reset Ball**: Center the ball and reverse its horizontal direction after a score.

- **Display**: Use Pygame's font system to render and display the scores.

Complete Pong Game Code

Combining all the steps, here's the complete Pong game code:

python

```python
import pygame

# Initialize Pygame
pygame.init()

# Screen dimensions
SCREEN_WIDTH = 800
SCREEN_HEIGHT = 600

# Colors (RGB)
WHITE = (255, 255, 255)
BLACK = (0, 0, 0)

# Paddle properties
PADDLE_WIDTH = 10
PADDLE_HEIGHT = 100
PADDLE_SPEED = 5
```

```python
# Ball properties
BALL_SIZE = 20
BALL_SPEED_X = 4
BALL_SPEED_Y = 4


# Set up the display
screen = pygame.display.set_mode((SCREEN_WIDTH,
SCREEN_HEIGHT))

pygame.display.set_caption("Pong Game")


# Define paddles and ball using pygame.Rect
left_paddle = pygame.Rect(50, SCREEN_HEIGHT//2
- PADDLE_HEIGHT//2, PADDLE_WIDTH,
PADDLE_HEIGHT)

right_paddle = pygame.Rect(SCREEN_WIDTH - 50 -
PADDLE_WIDTH, SCREEN_HEIGHT//2 -
PADDLE_HEIGHT//2, PADDLE_WIDTH,
PADDLE_HEIGHT)

ball = pygame.Rect(SCREEN_WIDTH//2 -
BALL_SIZE//2, SCREEN_HEIGHT//2 -
BALL_SIZE//2, BALL_SIZE, BALL_SIZE)


# Initialize scores
score_left = 0
```

```python
score_right = 0

# Initialize font
pygame.font.init()
font = pygame.font.SysFont(None, 36)

# Main game loop
running = True
clock = pygame.time.Clock()

while running:
    # Handle events
    for event in pygame.event.get():
        if event.type == pygame.QUIT:
            running = False

    # Get the state of all keyboard buttons
    keys = pygame.key.get_pressed()

    # Move left paddle (Player 1) using 'W' and 'S' keys
    if keys[pygame.K_w] and left_paddle.top > 0:
        left_paddle.y -= PADDLE_SPEED
```

```python
    if keys[pygame.K_s] and left_paddle.bottom <
SCREEN_HEIGHT:
        left_paddle.y += PADDLE_SPEED


    # Move right paddle (Player 2) using Up and Down
arrow keys
    if keys[pygame.K_UP] and right_paddle.top > 0:
        right_paddle.y -= PADDLE_SPEED
    if keys[pygame.K_DOWN] and right_paddle.bottom
< SCREEN_HEIGHT:
        right_paddle.y += PADDLE_SPEED


    # Move the ball
    ball.x += BALL_SPEED_X
    ball.y += BALL_SPEED_Y


    # Collision with top and bottom
    if ball.top <= 0 or ball.bottom >=
SCREEN_HEIGHT:
        BALL_SPEED_Y *= -1


    # Collision with paddles
    if ball.colliderect(left_paddle) or
ball.colliderect(right_paddle):
```

```python
        BALL_SPEED_X *= -1


    # Scoring
    if ball.left <= 0:
        score_right += 1
        # Reset ball to center
        ball.center = (SCREEN_WIDTH//2,
SCREEN_HEIGHT//2)
        BALL_SPEED_X *= -1  # Change direction


    if ball.right >= SCREEN_WIDTH:
        score_left += 1
        # Reset ball to center
        ball.center = (SCREEN_WIDTH//2,
SCREEN_HEIGHT//2)
        BALL_SPEED_X *= -1  # Change direction


    # Fill the screen with black
    screen.fill(BLACK)


    # Draw paddles and ball
    pygame.draw.rect(screen, WHITE, left_paddle)
    pygame.draw.rect(screen, WHITE, right_paddle)
```

```python
    pygame.draw.ellipse(screen, WHITE, ball)


    # Render scores
    score_text = font.render(f"{score_left}
{score_right}", True, WHITE)
    # Position the score at the top center
    screen.blit(score_text, (SCREEN_WIDTH//2 -
score_text.get_width()//2, 20))


    # Update the display
    pygame.display.flip()


    # Cap the frame rate
    clock.tick(60)


# Quit Pygame
pygame.quit()
```

Run this script to play the Pong game!

4.3 Adding Graphics and Sound

Enhancing your game with graphics and sound can make it more engaging and enjoyable. In this section, we'll add background images, customize paddles and ball visuals, and incorporate sound effects.

Step 1: Adding a Background Image

1. **Choose a Background Image**:

   - Select an image you'd like to use as the game's background (e.g., a simple sports court or abstract design).

   - Ensure the image is in the same directory as your game.py file and is in a compatible format (e.g., .png, .jpg).

2. **Load and Display the Background**:

python

```python
# Load the background image

background = pygame.image.load("background.png")

background = pygame.transform.scale(background, (SCREEN_WIDTH, SCREEN_HEIGHT))


# Inside the main game loop, replace
screen.fill(BLACK) with:

screen.blit(background, (0, 0))
```

Explanation:

- **Loading the Image**: Use pygame.image.load() to load the image file.

- **Scaling**: Adjust the image size to fit the game window using pygame.transform.scale().

- **Displaying**: Use screen.blit() to draw the image onto the screen.

Step 2: Customizing Paddles and Ball

Instead of simple shapes, you can use images for paddles and the ball.

1. **Prepare Paddle and Ball Images**:
   - Create or download images for the paddles and ball.
   - Save them in the game directory (e.g., paddle.png, ball.png).

2. **Load and Display Images**:

python

```
# Load paddle and ball images
paddle_image = pygame.image.load("paddle.png")
paddle_image =
pygame.transform.scale(paddle_image,
(PADDLE_WIDTH, PADDLE_HEIGHT))


ball_image = pygame.image.load("ball.png")
ball_image = pygame.transform.scale(ball_image,
(BALL_SIZE, BALL_SIZE))
```

```
# Inside the main game loop, replace
pygame.draw.rect and pygame.draw.ellipse with:
```

screen.blit(paddle_image, left_paddle)

screen.blit(paddle_image, right_paddle)

screen.blit(ball_image, ball)

Explanation:

- **Loading Images**: Similar to the background, load paddle and ball images.

- **Scaling**: Adjust their sizes to match the defined paddle and ball dimensions.

- **Displaying**: Use screen.blit() to draw the images at the positions of the paddles and ball.

Step 3: Adding Sound Effects

Sound effects enhance the gaming experience by providing audio feedback for actions like ball collisions and scoring.

1. **Prepare Sound Files**:
   - Obtain sound effects for ball hits and scoring (e.g., hit.wav, score.wav).
   - Ensure they are in the same directory as your game.py file.

2. **Load and Play Sounds**:

python

```
# Load sound effects
```

```python
hit_sound = pygame.mixer.Sound("hit.wav")
score_sound = pygame.mixer.Sound("score.wav")


# Play hit sound when ball collides with paddle or wall
if ball.colliderect(left_paddle) or
ball.colliderect(right_paddle):
    BALL_SPEED_X *= -1
    hit_sound.play()


if ball.top <= 0 or ball.bottom >= SCREEN_HEIGHT:
    BALL_SPEED_Y *= -1
    hit_sound.play()


# Play score sound when a player scores
if ball.left <= 0 or ball.right >= SCREEN_WIDTH:
    score_sound.play()
```

Explanation:

- **Loading Sounds**: Use pygame.mixer.Sound() to load sound files.
- **Playing Sounds**: Call the play() method on the sound objects when specific events occur (e.g., collisions, scoring).

Complete Pong Game with Graphics and Sound

Here's an updated version of the Pong game incorporating background, customized paddle and ball images, and sound effects:

python

```python
import pygame

# Initialize Pygame
pygame.init()

# Screen dimensions
SCREEN_WIDTH = 800
SCREEN_HEIGHT = 600

# Colors (RGB)
WHITE = (255, 255, 255)
BLACK = (0, 0, 0)

# Paddle properties
PADDLE_WIDTH = 20
PADDLE_HEIGHT = 100
PADDLE_SPEED = 5
```

```python
# Ball properties
BALL_SIZE = 20
BALL_SPEED_X = 4
BALL_SPEED_Y = 4


# Set up the display
screen = pygame.display.set_mode((SCREEN_WIDTH, SCREEN_HEIGHT))
pygame.display.set_caption("Pong Game with Graphics and Sound")


# Load images
background = pygame.image.load("background.png")
background = pygame.transform.scale(background, (SCREEN_WIDTH, SCREEN_HEIGHT))


paddle_image = pygame.image.load("paddle.png")
paddle_image = pygame.transform.scale(paddle_image, (PADDLE_WIDTH, PADDLE_HEIGHT))


ball_image = pygame.image.load("ball.png")
```

```python
ball_image = pygame.transform.scale(ball_image,
(BALL_SIZE, BALL_SIZE))


# Load sounds

pygame.mixer.init()

hit_sound = pygame.mixer.Sound("hit.wav")

score_sound = pygame.mixer.Sound("score.wav")


# Define paddles and ball using pygame.Rect

left_paddle = pygame.Rect(50, SCREEN_HEIGHT//2
- PADDLE_HEIGHT//2, PADDLE_WIDTH,
PADDLE_HEIGHT)

right_paddle = pygame.Rect(SCREEN_WIDTH - 50 -
PADDLE_WIDTH, SCREEN_HEIGHT//2 -
PADDLE_HEIGHT//2, PADDLE_WIDTH,
PADDLE_HEIGHT)

ball = pygame.Rect(SCREEN_WIDTH//2 -
BALL_SIZE//2, SCREEN_HEIGHT//2 -
BALL_SIZE//2, BALL_SIZE, BALL_SIZE)


# Initialize scores

score_left = 0

score_right = 0


# Initialize font
```

```python
pygame.font.init()
font = pygame.font.SysFont(None, 36)

# Main game loop
running = True
clock = pygame.time.Clock()

while running:
    # Handle events
    for event in pygame.event.get():
        if event.type == pygame.QUIT:
            running = False

    # Get the state of all keyboard buttons
    keys = pygame.key.get_pressed()

    # Move left paddle (Player 1) using 'W' and 'S' keys
    if keys[pygame.K_w] and left_paddle.top > 0:
        left_paddle.y -= PADDLE_SPEED
    if keys[pygame.K_s] and left_paddle.bottom < SCREEN_HEIGHT:
        left_paddle.y += PADDLE_SPEED
```

```python
    # Move right paddle (Player 2) using Up and Down
arrow keys

    if keys[pygame.K_UP] and right_paddle.top > 0:

        right_paddle.y -= PADDLE_SPEED

    if keys[pygame.K_DOWN] and right_paddle.bottom
< SCREEN_HEIGHT:

        right_paddle.y += PADDLE_SPEED


    # Move the ball

    ball.x += BALL_SPEED_X

    ball.y += BALL_SPEED_Y


    # Collision with top and bottom

    if ball.top <= 0 or ball.bottom >=
SCREEN_HEIGHT:

        BALL_SPEED_Y *= -1

        hit_sound.play()


    # Collision with paddles

    if ball.colliderect(left_paddle) or
ball.colliderect(right_paddle):

        BALL_SPEED_X *= -1
```

```python
        hit_sound.play()

    # Scoring
    if ball.left <= 0:
        score_right += 1
        score_sound.play()
        # Reset ball to center
        ball.center = (SCREEN_WIDTH//2,
SCREEN_HEIGHT//2)
        BALL_SPEED_X *= -1  # Change direction

    if ball.right >= SCREEN_WIDTH:
        score_left += 1
        score_sound.play()
        # Reset ball to center
        ball.center = (SCREEN_WIDTH//2,
SCREEN_HEIGHT//2)
        BALL_SPEED_X *= -1  # Change direction

    # Fill the screen with the background image
    screen.blit(background, (0, 0))

    # Draw paddles and ball
```

```python
    screen.blit(paddle_image, left_paddle)

    screen.blit(paddle_image, right_paddle)

    screen.blit(ball_image, ball)


    # Render scores

    score_text = font.render(f"{score_left}
{score_right}", True, WHITE)

    # Position the score at the top center

    screen.blit(score_text, (SCREEN_WIDTH//2 -
score_text.get_width()//2, 20))


    # Update the display

    pygame.display.flip()


    # Cap the frame rate

    clock.tick(60)


# Quit Pygame

pygame.quit()
```

Ensure that all image and sound files (background.png, paddle.png, ball.png, hit.wav, score.wav) are in the same directory as your Python script.

4.4 Enhancing Your Game with More Features

Now that you have a basic Pong game with graphics and sound, let's add some additional features to make it more dynamic and enjoyable.

Feature 1: Increasing Ball Speed After Each Hit

To make the game more challenging, you can increase the ball's speed each time it hits a paddle.

Implementation:

1. **Define Maximum Speed**:

python

```
MAX_SPEED = 10
```

2. **Update Ball Speed on Collision**:

python

```
# Collision with paddles
if ball.colliderect(left_paddle) or
ball.colliderect(right_paddle):

    BALL_SPEED_X *= -1

    hit_sound.play()


    # Increase speed
```

```python
if BALL_SPEED_X < 0 and abs(BALL_SPEED_X) < MAX_SPEED:
    BALL_SPEED_X -= 1
elif BALL_SPEED_X > 0 and abs(BALL_SPEED_X) < MAX_SPEED:
    BALL_SPEED_X += 1


if BALL_SPEED_Y < 0 and abs(BALL_SPEED_Y) < MAX_SPEED:
    BALL_SPEED_Y -= 1
elif BALL_SPEED_Y > 0 and abs(BALL_SPEED_Y) < MAX_SPEED:
    BALL_SPEED_Y += 1
```

Explanation:

- **MAX_SPEED**: Sets an upper limit to prevent the ball from becoming uncontrollable.

- **Speed Adjustment**: Incrementally increases the ball's speed after each paddle hit.

Feature 2: Displaying a Start Screen

Introduce a start screen that displays game instructions and waits for the player to begin.

Implementation:

1. **Create a Start Screen Function**:

python

```python
def start_screen():
    screen.blit(background, (0, 0))
    title_font = pygame.font.SysFont(None, 72)
    instruction_font = pygame.font.SysFont(None, 36)


    title_text = title_font.render("Welcome to Pong!",
True, WHITE)
    instruction_text = instruction_font.render("Press
SPACE to Start", True, WHITE)


    screen.blit(title_text, (SCREEN_WIDTH//2 -
title_text.get_width()//2, SCREEN_HEIGHT//2 - 100))
    screen.blit(instruction_text, (SCREEN_WIDTH//2 -
instruction_text.get_width()//2, SCREEN_HEIGHT//2))


    pygame.display.flip()


    waiting = True
    while waiting:
        for event in pygame.event.get():
            if event.type == pygame.QUIT:
                pygame.quit()
```

```
        exit()

    if event.type == pygame.KEYDOWN:

        if event.key == pygame.K_SPACE:

            waiting = False

    clock.tick(60)
```

2. **Call the Start Screen Before the Main Loop**:

python


```
start_screen()
```

Explanation:

- **Start Screen Function**: Displays a welcome message and waits for the player to press the SPACE key to start.

- **Event Handling**: Exits the game if the player closes the window or starts the game by pressing SPACE.

Feature 3: Adding Sound for Scoring and Paddle Hits

Enhance the auditory experience by differentiating sounds for scoring and paddle collisions.

Implementation:

1. **Prepare Additional Sound Files**:

    o   For example, paddle_hit.wav and score_point.wav.

2. **Load the New Sounds**:

python

```python
paddle_hit_sound =
pygame.mixer.Sound("paddle_hit.wav")

score_point_sound =
pygame.mixer.Sound("score_point.wav")
```

3. **Play Appropriate Sounds**:

python

```python
# Collision with paddles
if ball.colliderect(left_paddle) or
ball.colliderect(right_paddle):
    BALL_SPEED_X *= -1
    paddle_hit_sound.play()
    # Increase speed logic...


# Scoring
if ball.left <= 0:
    score_right += 1
    score_point_sound.play()
    # Reset ball logic...
```

```python
if ball.right >= SCREEN_WIDTH:

    score_left += 1

    score_point_sound.play()

    # Reset ball logic...
```

Explanation:

- **Distinct Sounds**: Use different sounds to signify different in-game events, enhancing player feedback.

Feature 4: Adding a Winning Condition

End the game when a player reaches a certain score, declaring them the winner.

Implementation:

1. **Define Winning Score**:

python

```python
WINNING_SCORE = 5
```

2. **Check for Winner After Scoring**:

python

```python
# After updating scores

if score_left >= WINNING_SCORE or score_right >= WINNING_SCORE:

    running = False
```

3. Display Winner Message After the Main Loop:

python

```python
# After the main loop ends
screen.blit(background, (0, 0))
winner_font = pygame.font.SysFont(None, 72)
if score_left >= WINNING_SCORE:
    winner_text = winner_font.render("Player 1 Wins!", True, WHITE)
else:
    winner_text = winner_font.render("Player 2 Wins!", True, WHITE)

screen.blit(winner_text, (SCREEN_WIDTH//2 - winner_text.get_width()//2, SCREEN_HEIGHT//2 - 50))
pygame.display.flip()

# Wait for a few seconds before quitting
pygame.time.delay(3000)
```

Explanation:

- **Winning Score**: Set a target score to determine the game's end.

- **Winner Announcement**: Display a message declaring the winning player before closing the game.

Complete Enhanced Pong Game Code

Combining all enhancements, here's the updated Pong game code:

python

```python
import pygame
import sys

# Initialize Pygame
pygame.init()

# Screen dimensions
SCREEN_WIDTH = 800
SCREEN_HEIGHT = 600

# Colors (RGB)
WHITE = (255, 255, 255)
BLACK = (0, 0, 0)

# Paddle properties
```

```python
PADDLE_WIDTH = 20
PADDLE_HEIGHT = 100
PADDLE_SPEED = 5


# Ball properties
BALL_SIZE = 20
BALL_SPEED_X = 4
BALL_SPEED_Y = 4
MAX_SPEED = 10


# Winning score
WINNING_SCORE = 5


# Set up the display
screen = pygame.display.set_mode((SCREEN_WIDTH, SCREEN_HEIGHT))
pygame.display.set_caption("Enhanced Pong Game")


# Load images
background = pygame.image.load("background.png")
background = pygame.transform.scale(background, (SCREEN_WIDTH, SCREEN_HEIGHT))
```

```python
paddle_image = pygame.image.load("paddle.png")

paddle_image =
pygame.transform.scale(paddle_image,
(PADDLE_WIDTH, PADDLE_HEIGHT))


ball_image = pygame.image.load("ball.png")

ball_image = pygame.transform.scale(ball_image,
(BALL_SIZE, BALL_SIZE))


# Load sounds

pygame.mixer.init()

paddle_hit_sound =
pygame.mixer.Sound("paddle_hit.wav")

score_point_sound =
pygame.mixer.Sound("score_point.wav")


# Define paddles and ball using pygame.Rect

left_paddle = pygame.Rect(50, SCREEN_HEIGHT//2
- PADDLE_HEIGHT//2, PADDLE_WIDTH,
PADDLE_HEIGHT)

right_paddle = pygame.Rect(SCREEN_WIDTH - 50 -
PADDLE_WIDTH, SCREEN_HEIGHT//2 -
PADDLE_HEIGHT//2, PADDLE_WIDTH,
PADDLE_HEIGHT)
```

```python
ball = pygame.Rect(SCREEN_WIDTH//2 -
BALL_SIZE//2, SCREEN_HEIGHT//2 -
BALL_SIZE//2, BALL_SIZE, BALL_SIZE)


# Initialize scores
score_left = 0
score_right = 0


# Initialize font
pygame.font.init()
font = pygame.font.SysFont(None, 36)


# Function to display the start screen
def start_screen():
    screen.blit(background, (0, 0))
    title_font = pygame.font.SysFont(None, 72)
    instruction_font = pygame.font.SysFont(None, 36)


    title_text = title_font.render("Welcome to Pong!",
True, WHITE)
    instruction_text = instruction_font.render("Press
SPACE to Start", True, WHITE)
```

```python
    screen.blit(title_text, (SCREEN_WIDTH//2 -
title_text.get_width()//2, SCREEN_HEIGHT//2 - 100))

    screen.blit(instruction_text, (SCREEN_WIDTH//2 -
instruction_text.get_width()//2, SCREEN_HEIGHT//2))


    pygame.display.flip()


    waiting = True
    while waiting:
        for event in pygame.event.get():
            if event.type == pygame.QUIT:
                pygame.quit()
                sys.exit()
            if event.type == pygame.KEYDOWN:
                if event.key == pygame.K_SPACE:
                    waiting = False
        pygame.time.Clock().tick(60)


# Display the start screen
start_screen()


# Main game loop
running = True
```

```python
clock = pygame.time.Clock()


while running:
    # Handle events
    for event in pygame.event.get():
        if event.type == pygame.QUIT:
            running = False


    # Get the state of all keyboard buttons
    keys = pygame.key.get_pressed()


    # Move left paddle (Player 1) using 'W' and 'S' keys
    if keys[pygame.K_w] and left_paddle.top > 0:
        left_paddle.y -= PADDLE_SPEED
    if keys[pygame.K_s] and left_paddle.bottom < SCREEN_HEIGHT:
        left_paddle.y += PADDLE_SPEED


    # Move right paddle (Player 2) using Up and Down arrow keys
    if keys[pygame.K_UP] and right_paddle.top > 0:
        right_paddle.y -= PADDLE_SPEED
```

```python
    if keys[pygame.K_DOWN] and right_paddle.bottom < SCREEN_HEIGHT:
        right_paddle.y += PADDLE_SPEED


    # Move the ball
    ball.x += BALL_SPEED_X
    ball.y += BALL_SPEED_Y


    # Collision with top and bottom
    if ball.top <= 0 or ball.bottom >= SCREEN_HEIGHT:
        BALL_SPEED_Y *= -1
        paddle_hit_sound.play()


    # Collision with paddles
    if ball.colliderect(left_paddle) or ball.colliderect(right_paddle):
        BALL_SPEED_X *= -1
        paddle_hit_sound.play()


        # Increase speed
        if BALL_SPEED_X < 0 and abs(BALL_SPEED_X) < MAX_SPEED:
```

```python
        BALL_SPEED_X -= 1
    elif BALL_SPEED_X > 0 and
abs(BALL_SPEED_X) < MAX_SPEED:
        BALL_SPEED_X += 1


    if BALL_SPEED_Y < 0 and
abs(BALL_SPEED_Y) < MAX_SPEED:
        BALL_SPEED_Y -= 1
    elif BALL_SPEED_Y > 0 and
abs(BALL_SPEED_Y) < MAX_SPEED:
        BALL_SPEED_Y += 1


    # Scoring
    if ball.left <= 0:
        score_right += 1
        score_point_sound.play()
        # Reset ball to center
        ball.center = (SCREEN_WIDTH//2,
SCREEN_HEIGHT//2)
        BALL_SPEED_X = 4  # Reset to initial speed
        BALL_SPEED_Y = 4


    if ball.right >= SCREEN_WIDTH:
```

```python
            score_left += 1
            score_point_sound.play()
            # Reset ball to center
            ball.center = (SCREEN_WIDTH//2,
SCREEN_HEIGHT//2)
            BALL_SPEED_X = -4  # Reset to initial speed
            BALL_SPEED_Y = -4


    # Check for winning condition
    if score_left >= WINNING_SCORE or score_right
>= WINNING_SCORE:
        running = False


    # Fill the screen with the background image
    screen.blit(background, (0, 0))


    # Draw paddles and ball
    screen.blit(paddle_image, left_paddle)
    screen.blit(paddle_image, right_paddle)
    screen.blit(ball_image, ball)


    # Render scores
```

```python
    score_text = font.render(f"{score_left}
{score_right}", True, WHITE)

    # Position the score at the top center

    screen.blit(score_text, (SCREEN_WIDTH//2 -
score_text.get_width()//2, 20))


    # Update the display

    pygame.display.flip()


    # Cap the frame rate

    clock.tick(60)


# Display the winner

screen.blit(background, (0, 0))

winner_font = pygame.font.SysFont(None, 72)

if score_left >= WINNING_SCORE:

    winner_text = winner_font.render("Player 1 Wins!",
True, WHITE)

else:

    winner_text = winner_font.render("Player 2 Wins!",
True, WHITE)
```

```
screen.blit(winner_text, (SCREEN_WIDTH//2 -
winner_text.get_width()//2, SCREEN_HEIGHT//2 -
50))
```

```
pygame.display.flip()
```

```
# Wait for a few seconds before quitting
```

```
pygame.time.delay(3000)
```

```
# Quit Pygame
```

```
pygame.quit()
```

*Ensure all additional sound and image files
(background.png, paddle.png, ball.png,
paddle_hit.wav, score_point.wav) are in the same
directory as your Python script.*

4.5 Exercise: Building Your Own Game

Now that you've learned how to create a Pong game,
it's time to apply your knowledge by building your own
simple game. Follow the steps below to create a basic
Catch the Falling Items game.

Project Overview

In this game, items will fall from the top of the screen,
and the player controls a basket at the bottom to

catch them. Each caught item increases the player's score, while missed items can either have no effect or decrease the score.

Step-by-Step Guide

Step 1: Setting Up the Game Window

1. **Create a New Python File**:

   - Name it catch_game.py.

2. **Initialize Pygame and Set Up the Display**:

python

```
import pygame
import random

pygame.init()

# Screen dimensions
SCREEN_WIDTH = 800
SCREEN_HEIGHT = 600

# Colors
WHITE = (255, 255, 255)
BLACK = (0, 0, 0)
RED = (255, 0, 0)
```

```python
GREEN = (0, 255, 0)
BLUE = (0, 0, 255)


# Set up the display
screen = pygame.display.set_mode((SCREEN_WIDTH, SCREEN_HEIGHT))
pygame.display.set_caption("Catch the Falling Items")


# Clock to control frame rate
clock = pygame.time.Clock()
```

Step 2: Creating the Player (Basket)

1. **Define Player Properties**:

python

```python
# Player (Basket) properties
basket_width = 100
basket_height = 20
basket_speed = 7


basket = pygame.Rect(SCREEN_WIDTH//2 - basket_width//2, SCREEN_HEIGHT - basket_height - 10, basket_width, basket_height)
```

2. **Draw the Basket**: Inside the main game loop, add:

python

```
pygame.draw.rect(screen, GREEN, basket)
```

Step 3: Creating Falling Items

1. **Define Item Properties and List**:

python

```
# Falling items
item_width = 30
item_height = 30
item_speed = 5
item_color = RED


items = []
spawn_event = pygame.USEREVENT + 1
pygame.time.set_timer(spawn_event, 1000)  # Spawn a new item every second
```

2. **Handle Spawning Items**:

python

```
for event in pygame.event.get():
```

```python
    if event.type == pygame.QUIT:

        running = False

    if event.type == spawn_event:

        item_x = random.randint(0, SCREEN_WIDTH -
item_width)

        item = pygame.Rect(item_x, 0, item_width,
item_height)

        items.append(item)
```

3. **Move and Draw Items**:

python

```python
for item in items[:]:

    item.y += item_speed

    pygame.draw.rect(screen, item_color, item)


    # Check if item is caught

    if item.colliderect(basket):

        items.remove(item)

        score += 1

        catch_sound.play()


    # Remove items that fall past the basket

    elif item.y > SCREEN_HEIGHT:
```

```python
        items.remove(item)
        miss_sound.play()
        score -= 1  # Optional: decrease score for
missed items
```

Step 4: Handling Player Movement

1. **Capture Keyboard Input:**

python

```python
keys = pygame.key.get_pressed()
if keys[pygame.K_LEFT] and basket.left > 0:
    basket.x -= basket_speed
if keys[pygame.K_RIGHT] and basket.right <
SCREEN_WIDTH:
    basket.x += basket_speed
```

Step 5: Displaying the Score

1. **Initialize Score and Font:**

python

```python
score = 0
font = pygame.font.SysFont(None, 36)
```

2. **Render and Display the Score:**

python

```python
score_text = font.render(f"Score: {score}", True,
WHITE)
```

```python
screen.blit(score_text, (10, 10))
```

Step 6: Adding Sound Effects

1. **Prepare Sound Files**:
   - catch.wav: Sound when an item is caught.
   - miss.wav: Sound when an item is missed.

2. **Load Sounds**:

python

```python
catch_sound = pygame.mixer.Sound("catch.wav")
miss_sound = pygame.mixer.Sound("miss.wav")
```

Step 7: Putting It All Together

Here is the complete catch_game.py script:

python

```python
import pygame
import random
import sys


# Initialize Pygame
```

```python
pygame.init()

# Screen dimensions
SCREEN_WIDTH = 800
SCREEN_HEIGHT = 600

# Colors
WHITE = (255, 255, 255)
BLACK = (0, 0, 0)
RED = (255, 0, 0)
GREEN = (0, 255, 0)

# Set up the display
screen = pygame.display.set_mode((SCREEN_WIDTH, SCREEN_HEIGHT))
pygame.display.set_caption("Catch the Falling Items")

# Clock to control frame rate
clock = pygame.time.Clock()

# Player (Basket) properties
basket_width = 100
```

```python
basket_height = 20

basket_speed = 7


basket = pygame.Rect(SCREEN_WIDTH//2 -
basket_width//2, SCREEN_HEIGHT - basket_height -
10, basket_width, basket_height)


# Falling items

item_width = 30

item_height = 30

item_speed = 5

item_color = RED


items = []

spawn_event = pygame.USEREVENT + 1

pygame.time.set_timer(spawn_event, 1000)  # Spawn
a new item every second


# Initialize score and font

score = 0

font = pygame.font.SysFont(None, 36)


# Load sounds
```

```python
pygame.mixer.init()
catch_sound = pygame.mixer.Sound("catch.wav")
miss_sound = pygame.mixer.Sound("miss.wav")


# Main game loop
running = True
while running:
    # Handle events
    for event in pygame.event.get():
        if event.type == pygame.QUIT:
            running = False
        if event.type == spawn_event:
            item_x = random.randint(0, SCREEN_WIDTH
- item_width)
            item = pygame.Rect(item_x, 0, item_width,
item_height)
            items.append(item)


    # Handle player movement
    keys = pygame.key.get_pressed()
    if keys[pygame.K_LEFT] and basket.left > 0:
        basket.x -= basket_speed
```

```python
    if keys[pygame.K_RIGHT] and basket.right <
SCREEN_WIDTH:
        basket.x += basket_speed

    # Move and draw items
    for item in items[:]:
        item.y += item_speed
        pygame.draw.rect(screen, item_color, item)

        # Check if item is caught
        if item.colliderect(basket):
            items.remove(item)
            score += 1
            catch_sound.play()

        # Remove items that fall past the basket
        elif item.y > SCREEN_HEIGHT:
            items.remove(item)
            miss_sound.play()
            score -= 1  # Optional: decrease score for
missed items

    # Fill the screen with black
```

```python
    screen.fill(BLACK)

    # Draw basket
    pygame.draw.rect(screen, GREEN, basket)

    # Draw items
    for item in items:
        pygame.draw.rect(screen, item_color, item)

    # Render and display the score
    score_text = font.render(f"Score: {score}", True,
WHITE)
    screen.blit(score_text, (10, 10))

    # Update the display
    pygame.display.flip()

    # Cap the frame rate
    clock.tick(60)

# Quit Pygame
pygame.quit()
```

```
sys.exit()
```

Ensure that all sound files (catch.wav, miss.wav) are in the same directory as your Python script.

Feature Enhancements

Once you've built the basic **Catch the Falling Items** game, consider adding the following features to enhance it further:

1. **Increasing Difficulty**:
   - Gradually increase the speed of falling items as the player's score increases.
   - Example:

python

```
if score % 5 == 0 and score != 0:
    item_speed += 1
```

2. **Multiple Item Types**:
   - Introduce different types of items with varying effects (e.g., bonus points, score penalties).
   - Use different colors or images to distinguish them.

3. **Lives System**:
   - Instead of decrementing the score for missed items, provide the player with a limited number of lives.

- Example:

python

```
lives = 3
# On miss
lives -= 1
if lives == 0:
    running = False
```

4. **High Score Tracking**:
    - Save and display the highest score achieved across game sessions.
    - Use file operations to store high scores.

5. **Visual Enhancements**:
    - Add animations for catching or missing items.
    - Implement particle effects or transitions.

6. **Sound Effects and Music**:
    - Incorporate background music to set the game's mood.
    - Add more diverse sound effects for different actions.

Exercise: Customize Your Catch Game

1. **Add Multiple Falling Item Types**:

- Create two types of items: one that increases the score and another that decreases it.

- Use different colors or shapes to represent each type.

2. **Implement a Lives System**:

- Start the player with 3 lives.

- Lose a life for each missed item instead of decrementing the score.

- Display remaining lives on the screen.

- End the game when lives reach zero.

3. **High Score Feature**:

- Save the highest score in a file named highscore.txt.

- Display the high score on the start and end screens.

4. **Add Background Music**:

- Load and play a looping background music track using pygame.mixer.music.

- Example:

python

```
pygame.mixer.music.load("background_music.mp3")

pygame.mixer.music.play(-1)  # -1 means the music will loop indefinitely
```

5. **Improve Graphics**:

   - Replace simple rectangles with images for the basket and items.

   - Animate the basket movement for smoother motion.

Challenge yourself to implement at least two of these features to enhance your game further!

Chapter 5: Building Interactive Applications

Welcome to **Chapter 5: Building Interactive Applications**! In this chapter, you'll learn how to create graphical user interfaces (GUIs) using Python's built-in library, **Tkinter**. GUIs allow users to interact with your programs through windows, buttons, text fields, and other visual elements, making your applications more user-friendly and engaging. We'll start with an introduction to GUI programming, explore the fundamental widgets like buttons and labels, develop a simple calculator app, and finally, expand your knowledge to build more complex applications. Let's dive in!

5.1 Introduction to GUI Programming with Tkinter

What is GUI Programming?

GUI Programming involves creating applications that users can interact with visually, using elements like windows, buttons, text fields, and more. Unlike command-line interfaces (CLIs), where users interact by typing commands, GUIs provide a more intuitive and accessible way to use software, especially for beginners.

What is Tkinter?

Tkinter is Python's standard library for creating graphical user interfaces. It comes bundled with most Python installations, meaning you don't need to install it separately. Tkinter provides a variety of widgets and tools to build windows, dialogs, buttons, labels, and other interactive components.

Why Use Tkinter?

- **Ease of Use**: Tkinter is straightforward and beginner-friendly, making it ideal for those new to GUI programming.

- **Cross-Platform**: Applications built with Tkinter run on Windows, macOS, and Linux without modification.

- **Integrated with Python**: As part of the standard library, Tkinter doesn't require additional installations.

- **Extensive Documentation and Community Support**: A wealth of tutorials, guides, and community forums are available to help you learn and troubleshoot.

Installing Tkinter

In most cases, Tkinter comes pre-installed with Python. To verify its installation:

1. **Open Your Python Interpreter**:

- o Open your terminal or command prompt.

- o Type python or python3 and press Enter.

2. **Import Tkinter**:

python

import tkinter

- o If no error appears, Tkinter is installed correctly.

- o If you encounter an error, you may need to install Tkinter separately. For example, on Debian-based Linux distributions:

bash

sudo apt-get install python3-tk

Setting Up a Basic Tkinter Application

Let's create a simple Tkinter window to get you started.

Step-by-Step Guide

1. **Create a New Python File**:

- o Open your IDE (e.g., Visual Studio Code).

- o Create a new file named gui_app.py.

2. **Write the Basic Tkinter Code**:

python

```python
import tkinter as tk

# Create the main window
root = tk.Tk()
root.title("My First Tkinter App")
root.geometry("400x300")  # Width x Height

# Run the application
root.mainloop()
```

3. **Run the Application**:

- o Save the gui_app.py file.
- o Run the script using your IDE or via the terminal:

bash

```bash
python gui_app.py
```

- o A window titled "My First Tkinter App" with dimensions 400x300 pixels should appear.

Congratulations! You've created your first Tkinter application.

5.2 Creating Buttons, Labels, and Input Fields

In this section, we'll explore some of Tkinter's fundamental widgets: **Labels**, **Buttons**, and **Entry** fields. These elements allow you to display text, create interactive buttons, and accept user input, respectively.

Labels

Labels are used to display text or images in your application.

Example: Creating and Displaying a Label

python

```
import tkinter as tk


# Create the main window
root = tk.Tk()
root.title("Labels Example")
root.geometry("400x300")
```

```python
# Create a label

greeting = tk.Label(root, text="Hello, Tkinter!",
font=("Arial", 24))

greeting.pack(pady=20)  # Adds vertical padding


# Run the application

root.mainloop()
```

Explanation:

- **tk.Label**: Initializes a label widget with the specified text and font.
- **pack()**: Adds the widget to the window. The pady parameter adds vertical padding for spacing.

Buttons

Buttons allow users to perform actions when clicked.

Example: Creating and Handling a Button

python

```python
import tkinter as tk


def on_button_click():
    greeting.config(text="Button Clicked!")
```

```python
# Create the main window
root = tk.Tk()
root.title("Buttons Example")
root.geometry("400x300")


# Create a label
greeting = tk.Label(root, text="Click the button
below:", font=("Arial", 16))
greeting.pack(pady=20)


# Create a button
button = tk.Button(root, text="Click Me",
command=on_button_click, font=("Arial", 14))
button.pack(pady=10)


# Run the application
root.mainloop()
```

Explanation:

- **tk.Button**: Initializes a button with the specified text and font.
- **command**: Specifies the function to call when the button is clicked.
- **on_button_click()**: Changes the label's text when the button is pressed.

Entry (Input) Fields

Entry widgets allow users to input text.

Example: Creating and Retrieving Input from an Entry Field

python

```python
import tkinter as tk

def show_input():
    user_input = entry.get()
    greeting.config(text=f"Hello, {user_input}!")

# Create the main window
root = tk.Tk()
root.title("Entry Example")
root.geometry("400x300")

# Create a label
prompt = tk.Label(root, text="Enter your name:",
font=("Arial", 16))
prompt.pack(pady=10)

# Create an entry field
```

```
entry = tk.Entry(root, font=("Arial", 14))

entry.pack(pady=5)


# Create a button to submit

submit_button = tk.Button(root, text="Submit",
command=show_input, font=("Arial", 14))

submit_button.pack(pady=10)


# Create a greeting label

greeting = tk.Label(root, text="", font=("Arial", 16))

greeting.pack(pady=20)


# Run the application

root.mainloop()
```

Explanation:

- **tk.Entry**: Initializes an entry widget for text input.

- **entry.get()**: Retrieves the current text from the entry field.

- **show_input()**: Updates the greeting label with the user's input when the submit button is clicked.

Layout Management: Pack, Grid, and Place

Tkinter provides three geometry managers to control the layout of widgets:

1. **Pack**: Organizes widgets in blocks before placing them in the parent widget.

2. **Grid**: Organizes widgets in a table-like structure with rows and columns.

3. **Place**: Places widgets at specific positions using absolute or relative coordinates.

Example: Using Grid for Layout

python

```python
import tkinter as tk


# Create the main window
root = tk.Tk()
root.title("Grid Layout Example")
root.geometry("400x300")


# Labels
label1 = tk.Label(root, text="Username:", font=("Arial", 14))
label2 = tk.Label(root, text="Password:", font=("Arial", 14))
```

```python
# Entry fields
entry1 = tk.Entry(root, font=("Arial", 14))
entry2 = tk.Entry(root, show="*", font=("Arial", 14))  # show="*" masks the input


# Button
login_button = tk.Button(root, text="Login", font=("Arial", 14))


# Arrange widgets using grid
label1.grid(row=0, column=0, padx=10, pady=10, sticky="e")
entry1.grid(row=0, column=1, padx=10, pady=10)
label2.grid(row=1, column=0, padx=10, pady=10, sticky="e")
entry2.grid(row=1, column=1, padx=10, pady=10)
login_button.grid(row=2, column=0, columnspan=2, pady=20)


# Run the application
root.mainloop()
```

Explanation:

- **grid(row, column)**: Places widgets in the specified row and column.

- **padx and pady**: Add horizontal and vertical padding, respectively.

- **sticky**: Aligns the widget within its grid cell ("e" for east/right alignment).

- **columnspan**: Allows the widget to span multiple columns.

Tip: Choose the geometry manager that best fits your application's layout needs. For more complex layouts, **Grid** is often more flexible than **Pack**.

Exercise: Creating Basic GUI Widgets

1. **Create a New Python File**:

   o   Name it basic_widgets.py.

2. **Design a Simple User Interface**:

   o   Add a label that says "Welcome to the App!"

   o   Add an entry field for the user to input their favorite color.

   o   Add a button labeled "Submit".

   o   When the button is clicked, update the label to say "Your favorite color is [color]."

3. **Run and Test Your Application**.

Example Solution:

python

```python
import tkinter as tk

def submit_color():
    color = color_entry.get()
    welcome_label.config(text=f"Your favorite color is {color}!")

# Create the main window
root = tk.Tk()
root.title("Favorite Color App")
root.geometry("400x300")

# Welcome label
welcome_label = tk.Label(root, text="Welcome to the App!", font=("Arial", 16))
welcome_label.pack(pady=20)

# Prompt label
prompt_label = tk.Label(root, text="Enter your favorite color:", font=("Arial", 14))
prompt_label.pack(pady=10)

# Entry field
```

```python
color_entry = tk.Entry(root, font=("Arial", 14))

color_entry.pack(pady=5)


# Submit button

submit_button = tk.Button(root, text="Submit",
command=submit_color, font=("Arial", 14))

submit_button.pack(pady=10)


# Run the application

root.mainloop()
```

Sample Interaction:

csharp

Welcome to the App!

Enter your favorite color: [User enters "Blue"]

[User clicks "Submit"]

Your favorite color is Blue!

5.3 Developing a Simple Calculator App

Building a calculator is a great way to practice GUI programming. In this section, we'll create a basic calculator that can perform addition, subtraction, multiplication, and division.

Step 1: Designing the Calculator Interface

We'll create buttons for digits (0-9), operations (+, -, *, /), a display label to show the input and results, and an equals (=) button to perform calculations.

Example: Calculator Layout

python

```python
import tkinter as tk

# Create the main window
root = tk.Tk()
root.title("Simple Calculator")
root.geometry("300x400")

# Display label
display = tk.Entry(root, font=("Arial", 24),
borderwidth=2, relief="groove")
display.pack(pady=20, padx=10, fill="x")

# Frame for buttons
button_frame = tk.Frame(root)
```

```
button_frame.pack(pady=10)

# Define buttons
buttons = [
    ('7', 1, 0), ('8', 1, 1), ('9', 1, 2), ('/', 1, 3),
    ('4', 2, 0), ('5', 2, 1), ('6', 2, 2), ('*', 2, 3),
    ('1', 3, 0), ('2', 3, 1), ('3', 3, 2), ('-', 3, 3),
    ('0', 4, 0), ('.', 4, 1), ('=', 4, 2), ('+', 4, 3),
]


for (text, row, column) in buttons:
    button = tk.Button(button_frame, text=text,
font=("Arial", 18), width=4, height=2)
    button.grid(row=row, column=column, padx=5,
pady=5)

# Run the application
root.mainloop()
```

Explanation:

- **tk.Entry**: Serves as the display for the calculator.

- **tk.Frame**: Groups buttons together.

- **Buttons Array**: Defines button labels and their grid positions.

- **Loop**: Creates buttons dynamically based on the buttons list.

Step 2: Implementing Button Functionality

To make the calculator operational, we'll define functions to handle button clicks, perform calculations, and update the display.

Example: Adding Functionality to Buttons

python

```python
import tkinter as tk


def button_click(value):
    current = display.get()
    display.delete(0, tk.END)
    display.insert(0, current + value)


def clear_display():
    display.delete(0, tk.END)


def calculate():
    try:
```

```python
        result = eval(display.get())
        display.delete(0, tk.END)
        display.insert(0, str(result))
    except Exception as e:
        display.delete(0, tk.END)
        display.insert(0, "Error")

# Create the main window
root = tk.Tk()
root.title("Simple Calculator")
root.geometry("300x400")

# Display label
display = tk.Entry(root, font=("Arial", 24),
borderwidth=2, relief="groove")
display.pack(pady=20, padx=10, fill="x")

# Frame for buttons
button_frame = tk.Frame(root)
button_frame.pack(pady=10)

# Define buttons with their actions
```

```python
buttons = [

    ('7', 1, 0, lambda: button_click('7')), ('8', 1, 1,
lambda: button_click('8')),

    ('9', 1, 2, lambda: button_click('9')), ('/', 1, 3,
lambda: button_click('/')),

    ('4', 2, 0, lambda: button_click('4')), ('5', 2, 1,
lambda: button_click('5')),

    ('6', 2, 2, lambda: button_click('6')), ('*', 2, 3,
lambda: button_click('*')),

    ('1', 3, 0, lambda: button_click('1')), ('2', 3, 1,
lambda: button_click('2')),

    ('3', 3, 2, lambda: button_click('3')), ('-', 3, 3,
lambda: button_click('-')),

    ('0', 4, 0, lambda: button_click('0')), ('.', 4, 1,
lambda: button_click('.')),

    ('=', 4, 2, calculate), ('+', 4, 3, lambda:
button_click('+')),

]


for (text, row, column, command) in buttons:
    button = tk.Button(button_frame, text=text,
font=("Arial", 18), width=4, height=2,
command=command)

    button.grid(row=row, column=column, padx=5,
pady=5)
```

```
# Clear button

clear_button = tk.Button(root, text="C", font=("Arial",
18), width=4, height=2, command=clear_display)

clear_button.pack(pady=5)


# Run the application

root.mainloop()
```

Explanation:

- **button_click()**: Appends the clicked button's value to the display.

- **clear_display()**: Clears the display when the "C" button is pressed.

- **calculate()**: Evaluates the expression in the display using eval(). Handles errors gracefully by displaying "Error" if the expression is invalid.

- **Buttons Array**: Now includes the command parameter to bind each button to its corresponding function.

- **"C" Button**: Added to clear the display.

Security Note: Using eval() can be dangerous if not handled properly, as it will execute any code passed to it. For a simple calculator, it's acceptable, but for more robust applications, consider using safer evaluation methods or parsing expressions manually.

Step 3: Enhancing the Calculator Interface

To improve usability, let's add a clear button (C) and ensure the calculator responds well to different window sizes.

Example: Improved Calculator Layout

python

```python
import tkinter as tk


def button_click(value):
    current = display.get()
    display.delete(0, tk.END)
    display.insert(0, current + value)


def clear_display():
    display.delete(0, tk.END)


def calculate():
    try:
        result = eval(display.get())
        display.delete(0, tk.END)
        display.insert(0, str(result))
    except Exception as e:
        display.delete(0, tk.END)
```

```python
        display.insert(0, "Error")


# Create the main window
root = tk.Tk()
root.title("Enhanced Calculator")
root.geometry("400x500")
root.resizable(False, False)  # Prevent resizing


# Display label
display = tk.Entry(root, font=("Arial", 24),
borderwidth=2, relief="groove", justify='right')
display.pack(pady=20, padx=20, fill="x")


# Frame for buttons
button_frame = tk.Frame(root)
button_frame.pack(pady=10)


# Define buttons with their actions
buttons = [
    ('7', 0, 0, lambda: button_click('7')), ('8', 0, 1,
lambda: button_click('8')),
    ('9', 0, 2, lambda: button_click('9')), ('/', 0, 3,
lambda: button_click('/')),
```

```python
    ('4', 1, 0, lambda: button_click('4')), ('5', 1, 1,
lambda: button_click('5')),

    ('6', 1, 2, lambda: button_click('6')), ('*', 1, 3,
lambda: button_click('*')),

    ('1', 2, 0, lambda: button_click('1')), ('2', 2, 1,
lambda: button_click('2')),

    ('3', 2, 2, lambda: button_click('3')), ('-', 2, 3,
lambda: button_click('-')),

    ('0', 3, 0, lambda: button_click('0')), ('.', 3, 1,
lambda: button_click('.')),

    ('=', 3, 2, calculate), ('+', 3, 3, lambda:
button_click('+')),

]


for (text, row, column, command) in buttons:
    button = tk.Button(button_frame, text=text,
font=("Arial", 18), width=5, height=2,
command=command)

    button.grid(row=row, column=column, padx=5,
pady=5)


# Clear button spanning two columns

clear_button = tk.Button(button_frame, text="C",
font=("Arial", 18), width=5, height=2,
command=clear_display, bg="lightgray")
```

```
clear_button.grid(row=4, column=0, columnspan=4,
pady=10)
```

```
# Run the application
```

```
root.mainloop()
```

Enhancements:

- **Window Size**: Increased to 400x500 pixels for better visibility.

- **Resizable**: Disabled resizing for consistent layout.

- **Justify**: Set justify='right' in the entry to align text to the right, mimicking standard calculators.

- **Clear Button**: Positioned below the main grid, spanning all columns for easy access.

Exercise: Building Your Own Calculator App

1. **Create a New Python File**:

   o Name it calculator_app.py.

2. **Design the Calculator Interface**:

   o Create a display entry at the top.

   o Arrange buttons for digits (0-9), operations (+, -, *, /), a clear button (C), and an equals button (=).

3. **Implement Functionality**:

- Clicking number and operation buttons appends to the display.
- Clicking C clears the display.
- Clicking = evaluates the expression and displays the result.

4. **Enhance Usability**:
   - Add keyboard support to allow users to type numbers and operations.
   - Implement error handling for invalid expressions.

Example Solution:

python

```python
import tkinter as tk


def button_click(value):
    current = display.get()
    display.delete(0, tk.END)
    display.insert(0, current + value)


def clear_display():
    display.delete(0, tk.END)
```

```python
def calculate(event=None):
    try:
        result = eval(display.get())
        display.delete(0, tk.END)
        display.insert(0, str(result))
    except Exception:
        display.delete(0, tk.END)
        display.insert(0, "Error")

# Create the main window
root = tk.Tk()
root.title("Calculator App")
root.geometry("400x500")
root.resizable(False, False)

# Display label
display = tk.Entry(root, font=("Arial", 24),
borderwidth=2, relief="groove", justify='right')
display.pack(pady=20, padx=20, fill="x")

# Frame for buttons
button_frame = tk.Frame(root)
```

```python
button_frame.pack(pady=10)


# Define buttons with their actions
buttons = [
    ('7', 0, 0, lambda: button_click('7')), ('8', 0, 1,
lambda: button_click('8')),

    ('9', 0, 2, lambda: button_click('9')), ('/', 0, 3,
lambda: button_click('/')),

    ('4', 1, 0, lambda: button_click('4')), ('5', 1, 1,
lambda: button_click('5')),

    ('6', 1, 2, lambda: button_click('6')), ('*', 1, 3,
lambda: button_click('*')),

    ('1', 2, 0, lambda: button_click('1')), ('2', 2, 1,
lambda: button_click('2')),

    ('3', 2, 2, lambda: button_click('3')), ('-', 2, 3,
lambda: button_click('-')),

    ('0', 3, 0, lambda: button_click('0')), ('.', 3, 1,
lambda: button_click('.')),

    ('=', 3, 2, calculate), ('+', 3, 3, lambda:
button_click('+')),

]


for (text, row, column, command) in buttons:
```

```python
    button = tk.Button(button_frame, text=text,
font=("Arial", 18), width=5, height=2,
command=command)

    button.grid(row=row, column=column, padx=5,
pady=5)


# Clear button

clear_button = tk.Button(button_frame, text="C",
font=("Arial", 18), width=5, height=2,
command=clear_display, bg="lightgray")

clear_button.grid(row=4, column=0, columnspan=4,
pady=10)


# Bind the Enter key to the calculate function

root.bind('<Return>', calculate)


# Run the application

root.mainloop()
```

Additional Enhancements:

- **Keyboard Support**: Users can press the Enter key to calculate the result.

- **Error Handling**: Displays "Error" for invalid expressions instead of crashing.

5.4 Expanding to More Complex Applications

Once you're comfortable with basic GUI elements and building simple applications, you can tackle more complex projects. This section provides ideas and guidance to help you advance your skills.

Project Ideas

1. **To-Do List Application**

   o **Features**:

      - Add, edit, and delete tasks.

      - Mark tasks as completed.

      - Save and load tasks from a file.

   o **Widgets Used**:

      - Labels, Buttons, Entry fields, Listboxes.

2. **Drawing App**

   o **Features**:

      - Draw freehand with the mouse.

      - Choose different colors and brush sizes.

      - Clear the canvas.

   o **Widgets Used**:

      - Canvas, Buttons, Color Chooser.

3. **Weather App**
    - **Features**:
        - Enter a city name to fetch current weather data.
        - Display temperature, humidity, and weather conditions.
    - **Widgets Used**:
        - Labels, Buttons, Entry fields.
    - **Additional Tools**:
        - Use an API (e.g., OpenWeatherMap) to retrieve weather data.
        - requests library for HTTP requests.

4. **Quiz Application**
    - **Features**:
        - Present multiple-choice questions.
        - Track and display the user's score.
        - Provide feedback for correct and incorrect answers.
    - **Widgets Used**:
        - Labels, Buttons, Radiobuttons.

5. **Expense Tracker**

- Features:
    - Add income and expense entries.
    - Categorize transactions.
    - Display a summary of finances.
  - Widgets Used:
    - Labels, Buttons, Entry fields, Treeview (from ttk for tables).

Utilizing Classes for Better Organization

As your applications grow in complexity, organizing your code using classes can make it more manageable and scalable.

Example: Refactoring the Calculator App Using a Class

python

```python
import tkinter as tk


class Calculator:
    def __init__(self, root):
        self.root = root
        self.root.title("Calculator App")
        self.root.geometry("400x500")
        self.root.resizable(False, False)
```

```python
        # Initialize expression
        self.expression = ""

        # Create display
        self.display = tk.Entry(root, font=("Arial", 24),
borderwidth=2, relief="groove", justify='right')
        self.display.pack(pady=20, padx=20, fill="x")

        # Create buttons
        self.create_buttons()

    def create_buttons(self):
        button_frame = tk.Frame(self.root)
        button_frame.pack(pady=10)

        buttons = [
            ('7', 0, 0, self.button_click), ('8', 0, 1,
self.button_click),
            ('9', 0, 2, self.button_click), ('/', 0, 3,
self.button_click),
            ('4', 1, 0, self.button_click), ('5', 1, 1,
self.button_click),
```

```python
        ('6', 1, 2, self.button_click), ('*', 1, 3,
self.button_click),

        ('1', 2, 0, self.button_click), ('2', 2, 1,
self.button_click),

        ('3', 2, 2, self.button_click), ('-', 2, 3,
self.button_click),

        ('0', 3, 0, self.button_click), ('.', 3, 1,
self.button_click),

        ('=', 3, 2, self.calculate), ('+', 3, 3,
self.button_click),

    ]


    for (text, row, column, command) in buttons:
        button = tk.Button(button_frame, text=text,
font=("Arial", 18), width=5, height=2,

                command=lambda x=text:
command(x))
        button.grid(row=row, column=column, padx=5,
pady=5)


    # Clear button

    clear_button = tk.Button(button_frame, text="C",
font=("Arial", 18), width=5, height=2,

                command=self.clear_display,
bg="lightgray")
```

```python
        clear_button.grid(row=4, column=0,
columnspan=4, pady=10)


    def button_click(self, value):
        self.expression += str(value)
        self.display.delete(0, tk.END)
        self.display.insert(tk.END, self.expression)


    def clear_display(self):
        self.expression = ""
        self.display.delete(0, tk.END)


    def calculate(self, _=None):
        try:
            result = eval(self.expression)
            self.display.delete(0, tk.END)
            self.display.insert(tk.END, str(result))
            self.expression = str(result)
        except Exception:
            self.display.delete(0, tk.END)
            self.display.insert(tk.END, "Error")
            self.expression = ""
```

```
# Create the main window
root = tk.Tk()
calc = Calculator(root)

# Bind Enter key to calculate
root.bind('<Return>', calc.calculate)

# Run the application
root.mainloop()
```

Explanation:

- **Calculator Class**: Encapsulates all functionalities of the calculator.

- **Methods**:

  - __init__: Initializes the calculator's interface and variables.

  - create_buttons: Dynamically creates buttons and assigns their commands.

  - button_click: Handles number and operation button clicks.

  - clear_display: Clears the display and resets the expression.

  - calculate: Evaluates the expression and updates the display.

- **Binding the Enter Key**: Allows users to press Enter to calculate the result, enhancing usability.

Benefits of Using Classes:

- **Organization**: Groups related functions and variables together.

- **Reusability**: Easier to reuse and extend functionalities.

- **Scalability**: Simplifies managing larger and more complex applications.

Exercise: Building a To-Do List Application

1. **Create a New Python File**:

   o Name it todo_app.py.

2. **Design the Interface**:

   o Add a label titled "To-Do List".

   o Add an entry field for adding new tasks.

   o Add a button labeled "Add Task".

   o Add a Listbox to display tasks.

   o Add a button labeled "Delete Selected".

3. **Implement Functionality**:

   o Clicking "Add Task" adds the entered task to the Listbox.

   o Selecting a task and clicking "Delete Selected" removes it from the Listbox.

- o   Optionally, save and load tasks from a file.

4. **Enhance Usability**:

- o   Allow pressing Enter to add a task.
- o   Add scrollbars if the task list becomes long.

Example Solution:

python

```python
import tkinter as tk
from tkinter import messagebox


class ToDoApp:
    def __init__(self, root):
        self.root = root
        self.root.title("To-Do List Application")
        self.root.geometry("400x500")
        self.root.resizable(False, False)


        # Title label
        title = tk.Label(root, text="To-Do List",
font=("Arial", 24))
        title.pack(pady=20)
```

```python
        # Frame for entry and add button
        input_frame = tk.Frame(root)
        input_frame.pack(pady=10)


        # Entry field
        self.task_entry = tk.Entry(input_frame,
font=("Arial", 14), width=25)
        self.task_entry.pack(side=tk.LEFT, padx=10)
        self.task_entry.bind('<Return>', self.add_task)


        # Add Task button
        add_button = tk.Button(input_frame, text="Add
Task", font=("Arial", 14), command=self.add_task)
        add_button.pack(side=tk.LEFT)


        # Listbox to display tasks
        self.tasks_listbox = tk.Listbox(root, font=("Arial",
14), selectmode=tk.SINGLE)
        self.tasks_listbox.pack(pady=20, padx=20,
fill=tk.BOTH, expand=True)


        # Scrollbar for Listbox
```

```python
        scrollbar = tk.Scrollbar(self.tasks_listbox)

        scrollbar.pack(side=tk.RIGHT, fill=tk.Y)

        self.tasks_listbox.config(yscrollcommand=scrollbar.se
t)

        scrollbar.config(command=self.tasks_listbox.yview)


        # Delete Task button
        delete_button = tk.Button(root, text="Delete
Selected", font=("Arial", 14),
command=self.delete_task)

        delete_button.pack(pady=10)


    def add_task(self, event=None):
        task = self.task_entry.get().strip()
        if task:
            self.tasks_listbox.insert(tk.END, task)
            self.task_entry.delete(0, tk.END)
        else:
            messagebox.showwarning("Input Error",
"Please enter a task.")


    def delete_task(self):
```

```
        selected_index = self.tasks_listbox.curselection()

        if selected_index:

            self.tasks_listbox.delete(selected_index)

        else:

            messagebox.showwarning("Selection Error",
"Please select a task to delete.")


# Create the main window

root = tk.Tk()

app = ToDoApp(root)


# Run the application

root.mainloop()
```

Explanation:

- **ToDoApp Class**: Encapsulates the to-do list application's functionalities.

- **Widgets**:

    o **Entry Field**: For inputting new tasks.

    o **Add Task Button**: Adds the task to the Listbox.

    o **Listbox**: Displays the list of tasks.

    o **Delete Selected Button**: Removes the selected task from the Listbox.

- ○ **Scrollbar**: Allows scrolling through the task list.

- **Event Binding**: Pressing Enter in the entry field triggers the add_task method.

- **Error Handling**: Warns the user if attempting to add an empty task or delete without selecting.

Optional Enhancements:

- **Save and Load Tasks**: Persist tasks by saving them to a file and loading them when the application starts.

- **Task Completion**: Allow marking tasks as completed (e.g., changing their color or adding a checkmark).

Chapter 6: Introduction to Data Visualization

Welcome to **Chapter 6: Introduction to Data Visualization**! Data visualization is a powerful tool that transforms raw data into meaningful insights through visual representations. Whether you're analyzing sports statistics, tracking your gaming scores, or exploring academic performance, visualizing data can help you understand patterns, trends, and outliers more effectively. In this chapter, we'll delve into the fundamentals of data visualization, explore how to create various charts using **Matplotlib**, build interactive visuals with **Plotly**, and work on real-world data projects to solidify your understanding. Let's embark on this visual journey!

6.1 Understanding Data Visualization

What is Data Visualization?

Data Visualization is the graphical representation of information and data. By using visual elements like charts, graphs, and maps, data visualization tools provide an accessible way to see and understand trends, outliers, and patterns in data.

Why is Data Visualization Important?

- **Simplifies Complex Data**: Transforms large datasets into understandable visual formats.

- **Identifies Patterns and Trends**: Helps in recognizing trends, correlations, and anomalies.

- **Enhances Decision Making**: Facilitates informed decisions based on visual insights.

- **Improves Communication**: Makes it easier to convey information to others effectively.

- **Engages the Audience**: Visuals are often more engaging than raw data, making presentations more compelling.

Types of Data Visualizations

1. **Bar Charts**: Compare quantities across different categories.

2. **Line Charts**: Show trends over time.

3. **Pie Charts**: Display proportions of a whole.

4. **Histograms**: Illustrate the distribution of numerical data.

5. **Scatter Plots**: Show relationships between two variables.

6. **Heatmaps**: Represent data values through variations in color.

7. **Box Plots**: Summarize data distributions with quartiles.

8. **Geographical Maps**: Visualize data across different regions.

Principles of Effective Data Visualization

- **Clarity**: Ensure that the visualization is easy to understand.

- **Accuracy**: Represent data truthfully without distortion.

- **Simplicity**: Avoid unnecessary complexity; focus on essential information.

- **Consistency**: Use consistent colors, scales, and styles.

- **Relevance**: Choose visualization types that best represent the data and insights you aim to convey.

Tools for Data Visualization in Python

- **Matplotlib**: A versatile library for creating static, animated, and interactive visualizations.

- **Seaborn**: Built on Matplotlib, it provides a high-level interface for attractive statistical graphics.

- **Plotly**: Offers interactive, web-based visualizations.

- **Pandas Visualization**: Built-in plotting capabilities using Matplotlib.

In this chapter, we'll focus on **Matplotlib** and **Plotly** to create both static and interactive visualizations.

6.2 Creating Charts with Matplotlib

Matplotlib is one of the most widely used libraries for data visualization in Python. It offers a variety of plotting functions and customization options, making it suitable for both beginners and advanced users.

Installing Matplotlib

Matplotlib is often included with Python distributions like Anaconda. To install it using pip, run:

bash

```
pip install matplotlib
```

Importing Matplotlib

It's common practice to import Matplotlib's pyplot module with the alias plt:

python

```
import matplotlib.pyplot as plt
```

Basic Plotting with Matplotlib

Let's start by creating a simple line chart.

Example 1: Line Chart

python

```python
import matplotlib.pyplot as plt

# Sample data
years = [2015, 2016, 2017, 2018, 2019, 2020]
sales = [250, 300, 400, 350, 500, 450]

# Create a line chart
plt.plot(years, sales, marker='o', linestyle='-', color='b')

# Add title and labels
plt.title('Annual Sales')
plt.xlabel('Year')
plt.ylabel('Sales (in USD)')

# Show the plot
plt.show()
```

Output:

Explanation:

- **plt.plot()**: Plots the data with specified markers, line style, and color.

- **plt.title(), plt.xlabel(), plt.ylabel()**: Add a title and axis labels.

- **plt.show()**: Displays the plot.

Example 2: Bar Chart

python

```python
import matplotlib.pyplot as plt


# Sample data
categories = ['Python', 'Java', 'C++', 'JavaScript', 'Ruby']
popularity = [45, 30, 25, 35, 20]


# Create a bar chart
plt.bar(categories, popularity, color='skyblue')


# Add title and labels
plt.title('Programming Language Popularity')
plt.xlabel('Languages')
plt.ylabel('Popularity (%)')


# Show the plot
plt.show()
```

Output:

Explanation:

- **plt.bar()**: Creates a vertical bar chart with specified colors.

- The rest follows similarly to the line chart.

Example 3: Pie Chart

python

```
import matplotlib.pyplot as plt


# Sample data
labels = ['Python', 'Java', 'C++', 'JavaScript', 'Ruby']
sizes = [45, 30, 15, 7, 3]
colors = ['gold', 'yellowgreen', 'lightcoral',
'lightskyblue', 'lightgreen']
explode = (0.1, 0, 0, 0, 0)  # Explode the first slice


# Create a pie chart
plt.pie(sizes, explode=explode, labels=labels,
colors=colors,
       autopct='%1.1f%%', shadow=True,
startangle=140)
```

```python
plt.title('Programming Language Distribution')

plt.axis('equal')  # Equal aspect ratio ensures the pie
chart is circular.

plt.show()
```

Output:

Explanation:

- **plt.pie()**: Creates a pie chart with specified parameters.

- **autopct**: Displays the percentage on each slice.

- **explode**: Separates the first slice for emphasis.

- **plt.axis('equal')**: Ensures the pie chart is a circle.

Customizing Plots

Matplotlib offers extensive customization options to enhance your visualizations.

Adding Gridlines

python

```python
import matplotlib.pyplot as plt


# Sample data
months = ['Jan', 'Feb', 'Mar', 'Apr', 'May', 'Jun']
```

```
revenue = [5000, 7000, 8000, 6000, 7500, 9000]


plt.plot(months, revenue, marker='s', linestyle='--',
color='r')
plt.title('Monthly Revenue')
plt.xlabel('Month')
plt.ylabel('Revenue (USD)')
plt.grid(True)  # Adds gridlines
plt.show()
```

Changing Ticks and Limits

python

```
import matplotlib.pyplot as plt


# Sample data
days = [1, 2, 3, 4, 5, 6, 7]
temperatures = [22, 24, 19, 23, 25, 20, 18]


plt.plot(days, temperatures, marker='^', color='m')
plt.title('Weekly Temperatures')
plt.xlabel('Day')
plt.ylabel('Temperature (°C)')
```

```python
# Set x and y limits
plt.xlim(0, 8)
plt.ylim(15, 26)

# Customize ticks
plt.xticks(days)
plt.yticks(range(15, 27, 2))

plt.grid(True)
plt.show()
```

Adding Legends

python

```python
import matplotlib.pyplot as plt

# Sample data
x = [0, 1, 2, 3, 4, 5]
y1 = [0, 1, 4, 9, 16, 25]
y2 = [0, 1, 8, 27, 64, 125]

plt.plot(x, y1, label='Squares', marker='o')
```

```python
plt.plot(x, y2, label='Cubes', marker='s')

plt.title('Squares vs. Cubes')

plt.xlabel('Number')

plt.ylabel('Value')

plt.legend()  # Adds a legend

plt.grid(True)

plt.show()
```

Saving Plots

You can save your plots in various formats like PNG, JPEG, PDF, etc.

python

```python
import matplotlib.pyplot as plt


# Sample data
x = [1, 2, 3, 4, 5]
y = [10, 20, 25, 30, 40]


plt.plot(x, y, marker='d', color='g')
plt.title('Sample Plot')
plt.xlabel('X-axis')
```

```
plt.ylabel('Y-axis')

plt.grid(True)


# Save the plot as a PNG file

plt.savefig('sample_plot.png')


plt.show()
```

Explanation:

- **plt.savefig()**: Saves the current figure to a file. Specify the desired format by the file extension.

Exercise: Creating Your Own Charts

1. **Line Chart Exercise**:

   ○ Create a line chart showing the number of hours you studied each week for six weeks.

   ○ Customize the line with a different color and marker.

   ○ Add appropriate titles and labels.

2. **Bar Chart Exercise**:

   ○ Plot a bar chart representing the number of games you played each month.

   ○ Use different colors for each bar.

- Include a legend if you categorize games.

3. **Pie Chart Exercise**:

  - Create a pie chart showing the distribution of time spent on different activities (e.g., gaming, studying, exercising).

  - Explode the slice representing the activity you spend the most time on.

  - Add percentage labels to each slice.

Example Solutions:

Line Chart Solution:

python

```
import matplotlib.pyplot as plt


# Data
weeks = [1, 2, 3, 4, 5, 6]
study_hours = [5, 7, 6, 8, 7, 9]


# Plot
plt.plot(weeks, study_hours, marker='o', linestyle='-', color='purple')
plt.title('Weekly Study Hours')
```

```
plt.xlabel('Week')

plt.ylabel('Hours Studied')

plt.grid(True)

plt.show()
```

Bar Chart Solution:

python

```
import matplotlib.pyplot as plt


# Data

months = ['January', 'February', 'March', 'April', 'May',
'June']

games_played = [12, 15, 10, 20, 18, 25]


# Plot

plt.bar(months, games_played, color=['red', 'blue',
'green', 'orange', 'purple', 'cyan'])

plt.title('Games Played Each Month')

plt.xlabel('Month')

plt.ylabel('Number of Games')

plt.show()
```

Pie Chart Solution:

python

```python
import matplotlib.pyplot as plt

# Data
activities = ['Gaming', 'Studying', 'Exercising',
'Reading']
time_spent = [40, 30, 20, 10]
colors = ['gold', 'lightblue', 'lightgreen', 'lightcoral']
explode = (0.1, 0, 0, 0)  # Explode the first slice

# Plot
plt.pie(time_spent, explode=explode, labels=activities,
colors=colors,
    autopct='%1.1f%%', shadow=True,
startangle=140)
plt.title('Time Spent on Activities')
plt.axis('equal')
plt.show()
```

6.3 Interactive Visuals with Plotly

While Matplotlib excels at creating static
visualizations, **Plotly** is a powerful library for building
interactive charts that can be embedded in web

applications or viewed in Jupyter notebooks. Interactive visuals enhance user engagement by allowing dynamic exploration of data.

Installing Plotly

To install Plotly, use pip:

bash

```
pip install plotly
```

Importing Plotly

Import Plotly's graph_objects module with the alias go:

python

```
import plotly.graph_objects as go
```

Basic Plotting with Plotly

Let's create an interactive line chart.

Example 1: Interactive Line Chart

python

```
import plotly.graph_objects as go

# Sample data
years = [2015, 2016, 2017, 2018, 2019, 2020]
```

```python
sales = [250, 300, 400, 350, 500, 450]

# Create a line chart
fig = go.Figure(data=go.Scatter(x=years, y=sales,
mode='lines+markers', name='Sales'))

# Add titles and labels
fig.update_layout(title='Annual Sales',
            xaxis_title='Year',
            yaxis_title='Sales (in USD)')

# Show the plot
fig.show()
```

Output:

An interactive line chart where you can hover over points to see details, zoom in/out, and toggle data series.

Example 2: Interactive Bar Chart

python

```python
import plotly.graph_objects as go

# Sample data
```

```python
categories = ['Python', 'Java', 'C++', 'JavaScript',
'Ruby']
popularity = [45, 30, 25, 35, 20]


# Create a bar chart
fig = go.Figure(data=go.Bar(x=categories,
y=popularity, marker_color='indianred'))


# Add titles and labels
fig.update_layout(title='Programming Language
Popularity',

                xaxis_title='Languages',

                yaxis_title='Popularity (%)')


# Show the plot
fig.show()
```

Example 3: Interactive Scatter Plot

python

```python
import plotly.graph_objects as go


# Sample data
hours_studied = [5, 7, 6, 8, 7, 9]
```

```
grades = [75, 85, 80, 90, 88, 95]


# Create a scatter plot

fig = go.Figure(data=go.Scatter(x=hours_studied,
y=grades, mode='markers',

                    marker=dict(size=12,
color='blue'),

                    text=['Week 1', 'Week 2', 'Week
3', 'Week 4', 'Week 5', 'Week 6'],

                    name='Grades'))


# Add titles and labels

fig.update_layout(title='Study Hours vs. Grades',

            xaxis_title='Hours Studied',

            yaxis_title='Grade')


# Show the plot

fig.show()
```

Explanation:

- **Interactive Elements**: Hover tooltips,
  zooming, panning, and clickable legends
  enhance data exploration.

- **Customization**: Plotly offers extensive customization options similar to Matplotlib but with added interactivity.

Plotly Express: A Simplified Interface

Plotly Express is a high-level interface for Plotly that simplifies the creation of complex plots with less code.

Installing Plotly Express

Plotly Express is included in the Plotly library. Ensure you have Plotly installed:

bash

```
pip install plotly
```

Importing Plotly Express

python

```
import plotly.express as px
```

Example: Creating a Scatter Plot with Plotly Express

python

```
import plotly.express as px

# Sample data
df = {
```

```python
    'Hours Studied': [5, 7, 6, 8, 7, 9],

    'Grade': [75, 85, 80, 90, 88, 95],

    'Week': ['Week 1', 'Week 2', 'Week 3', 'Week 4',
'Week 5', 'Week 6']

}


# Create a scatter plot

fig = px.scatter(df, x='Hours Studied', y='Grade',
text='Week',

        title='Study Hours vs. Grades',

        labels={'Hours Studied': 'Hours Studied',
'Grade': 'Grade'},

        template='plotly_dark')


# Show the plot

fig.show()
```

Explanation:

- **px.scatter()**: Simplifies scatter plot creation with data mapping.
- **template**: Applies a predefined theme to the plot.

Customizing Interactive Plots

Plotly allows extensive customization to enhance the visual appeal and functionality of your charts.

Example: Adding Annotations and Styling

python

```python
import plotly.graph_objects as go

# Sample data
categories = ['Python', 'Java', 'C++', 'JavaScript', 'Ruby']
popularity = [45, 30, 25, 35, 20]

# Create a bar chart
fig = go.Figure(data=go.Bar(x=categories, y=popularity, marker_color='lightsalmon'))

# Add titles and labels
fig.update_layout(title='Programming Language Popularity',
                  xaxis_title='Languages',
                  yaxis_title='Popularity (%)',
                  plot_bgcolor='rgba(0,0,0,0)')  # Transparent background

# Add annotations
```

```python
for i, v in enumerate(popularity):
    fig.add_annotation(x=categories[i], y=v + 1,
                text=str(v),
                showarrow=False,
                font=dict(color='black', size=12))


# Show the plot
fig.show()
```

Explanation:

- **plot_bgcolor**: Changes the plot background color.

- **fig.add_annotation()**: Adds text annotations above each bar.

Saving Interactive Plots

You can save Plotly figures as HTML files, allowing them to be viewed in web browsers or embedded in websites.

python

```python
import plotly.graph_objects as go


# Sample data
x = [1, 2, 3, 4, 5]
```

```
y = [10, 15, 13, 17, 14]


# Create a line chart
fig = go.Figure(data=go.Scatter(x=x, y=y,
mode='lines+markers', name='Data'))


# Add titles and labels
fig.update_layout(title='Interactive Line Chart',
                xaxis_title='X-axis',
                yaxis_title='Y-axis')


# Save the plot as an HTML file
fig.write_html('interactive_line_chart.html')


# Show the plot
fig.show()
```

Explanation:

- **fig.write_html()**: Saves the figure as an HTML file, preserving interactivity.

Exercise: Creating Interactive Charts

1. **Interactive Bar Chart Exercise**:

- Create an interactive bar chart showing the number of games played each day of the week.

- Add hover tooltips displaying the exact number of games.

- Customize the colors and add a title.

2. **Interactive Scatter Plot Exercise**:

- Plot a scatter plot representing the relationship between hours studied and grades achieved over six weeks.

- Include hover labels indicating the week number.

- Add a trendline to visualize the correlation.

3. **Interactive Pie Chart Exercise**:

- Create an interactive pie chart showing the distribution of your time spent on various activities (e.g., gaming, studying, exercising, reading).

- Add hover information to display percentages.

- Explode the slice representing the activity you spend the most time on.

Example Solutions:

Interactive Bar Chart Solution:

python

```python
import plotly.graph_objects as go

# Data
days = ['Monday', 'Tuesday', 'Wednesday', 'Thursday',
'Friday', 'Saturday', 'Sunday']

games_played = [4, 6, 5, 7, 3, 8, 2]


# Create a bar chart
fig = go.Figure(data=go.Bar(x=days,
y=games_played, marker_color='lightskyblue'))


# Add titles and labels
fig.update_layout(title='Games Played Each Day',

                xaxis_title='Day of the Week',

                yaxis_title='Number of Games')


# Add hover information
fig.update_traces(hovertemplate='Games Played:
%{y}')


# Show the plot
fig.show()
```

Interactive Scatter Plot Solution:

python

```python
import plotly.express as px

# Data
df = {
    'Hours Studied': [5, 7, 6, 8, 7, 9],
    'Grades': [75, 85, 80, 90, 88, 95],
    'Week': ['Week 1', 'Week 2', 'Week 3', 'Week 4',
'Week 5', 'Week 6']
}

# Create a scatter plot with trendline
fig = px.scatter(df, x='Hours Studied', y='Grades',
text='Week',
                 title='Hours Studied vs. Grades Achieved',
                 labels={'Hours Studied': 'Hours Studied',
'Grades': 'Grades'},
                 trendline='ols',  # Ordinary Least Squares
trendline
                 template='plotly_white')
```

```python
# Customize hover information
fig.update_traces(mode='markers+text',
textposition='top center')


# Show the plot
fig.show()
```

Interactive Pie Chart Solution:

python


```python
import plotly.graph_objects as go


# Data
activities = ['Gaming', 'Studying', 'Exercising',
'Reading']

time_spent = [40, 30, 20, 10]

colors = ['#636EFA', '#EF553B', '#00CC96',
'#AB63FA']

explode = (0.1, 0, 0, 0)  # Explode the first slice


# Create a pie chart
fig = go.Figure(data=[go.Pie(labels=activities,
values=time_spent, hole=.3,

                    marker=dict(colors=colors),
```

```
                  hoverinfo='label+percent',

                  textinfo='label+percent',

                  textfont_size=20,

                  sort=False,

                  explode=explode)])


# Add title

fig.update_layout(title_text='Time Spent on Activities')


# Show the plot

fig.show()
```

6.4 Real-World Data Projects

Applying data visualization skills to real-world projects solidifies your understanding and showcases your abilities. Here are some project ideas that integrate data visualization using Matplotlib and Plotly.

Project 1: Analyzing Sports Statistics

Objective: Visualize and analyze the performance of your favorite sports team or player.

Steps:

1. **Data Collection**:

- o Gather data on games played, points scored, assists, rebounds, etc.
- o Use websites like NBA Stats or ESPN for sports data.

2. **Data Preparation**:

- o Organize the data into a structured format (e.g., CSV, Excel).
- o Clean and preprocess the data using Pandas.

3. **Visualization**:

- o Create line charts showing performance over time.
- o Use bar charts to compare different players or metrics.
- o Develop interactive dashboards with Plotly for dynamic exploration.

4. **Analysis**:

- o Identify trends, peak performance periods, and areas for improvement.
- o Present insights through your visualizations.

Example:

Visualize a basketball player's points per game over a season using Matplotlib.

python

```python
import matplotlib.pyplot as plt

# Sample data
games = list(range(1, 21))
points = [22, 25, 19, 24, 30, 28, 26, 25, 27, 29, 31, 24,
22, 23, 25, 28, 30, 27, 26, 29]


plt.plot(games, points, marker='o', linestyle='-',
color='green')
plt.title('Player Points per Game')
plt.xlabel('Game Number')
plt.ylabel('Points Scored')
plt.grid(True)
plt.show()
```

Project 2: Visualizing Academic Performance

Objective: Track and visualize your academic performance across different subjects and semesters.

Steps:

1. **Data Collection**:
    - Record your grades for each subject per semester.
    - Optionally, include additional data like study hours, attendance, etc.

2. **Data Preparation**:

   o Structure the data in a DataFrame using Pandas.

   o Handle missing values and ensure data consistency.

3. **Visualization**:

   o Use bar charts to compare grades across subjects.

   o Create line charts to observe performance trends over semesters.

   o Develop a dashboard with multiple charts using Plotly for comprehensive analysis.

4. **Analysis**:

   o Identify subjects where you're excelling or need improvement.

   o Correlate study habits with academic outcomes.

Example:

Create a bar chart comparing grades across subjects.

python

```
import matplotlib.pyplot as plt


# Sample data
```

```
subjects = ['Mathematics', 'Physics', 'Chemistry',
'Biology', 'English']

grades = [88, 92, 79, 85, 90]


plt.bar(subjects, grades, color='skyblue')

plt.title('Academic Grades by Subject')

plt.xlabel('Subjects')

plt.ylabel('Grades')

plt.ylim(70, 100)

plt.show()
```

Project 3: Tracking Personal Habits

Objective: Monitor and visualize your daily habits to understand patterns and make improvements.

Steps:

1. **Data Collection**:
   - Track habits such as hours of sleep, exercise, screen time, etc., daily.
   - Use a spreadsheet or a simple database to log data.

2. **Data Preparation**:
   - Organize the data for easy analysis.
   - Use Pandas to clean and preprocess.

3. **Visualization**:

- Create histograms to view distributions (e.g., hours of sleep).

- Use scatter plots to explore correlations (e.g., exercise hours vs. mood).

- Develop interactive visuals with Plotly to filter data by weeks or months.

4. **Analysis**:

- Discover patterns and habits that positively or negatively impact your well-being.

- Set goals based on your findings.

Example:

Visualize the relationship between hours of exercise and mood ratings.

python

```
import plotly.express as px


# Sample data
data = {
    'Exercise Hours': [0, 1, 2, 3, 4, 1.5, 2.5, 3.5, 0.5, 2],
    'Mood Rating': [5, 6, 7, 8, 9, 6.5, 7.5, 8.5, 5.5, 7]
}
```

```
fig = px.scatter(data, x='Exercise Hours', y='Mood
Rating',

        title='Exercise vs. Mood',

        labels={'Exercise Hours': 'Hours of
Exercise', 'Mood Rating': 'Mood Rating'},

        trendline='ols')


fig.show()
```

Project 4: Visualizing Financial Data

Objective: Analyze and visualize your personal finances to manage expenses and savings effectively.

Steps:

1. **Data Collection**:
   - Track income, expenses, savings, and investments.
   - Categorize expenses (e.g., food, entertainment, transportation).

2. **Data Preparation**:
   - Organize data into categories and time frames (monthly, yearly).
   - Use Pandas for data manipulation.

3. **Visualization**:
   - Create pie charts to show expense distribution.

- o Use line charts to track income and savings growth over time.

- o Develop interactive dashboards with multiple charts for comprehensive financial overview.

4. **Analysis**:

- o Identify spending patterns.

- o Set budgeting goals and monitor progress.

Example:

Create a pie chart showing the distribution of monthly expenses.

python

```
import matplotlib.pyplot as plt


# Sample data
categories = ['Rent', 'Food', 'Transportation', 'Entertainment', 'Utilities', 'Others']
expenses = [1200, 600, 300, 150, 200, 250]
colors = ['gold', 'lightcoral', 'lightskyblue', 'lightgreen', 'violet', 'lightgrey']
explode = (0.1, 0, 0, 0, 0, 0)  # Explode the first slice
```

```
plt.pie(expenses, explode=explode,
labels=categories, colors=colors,

    autopct='%1.1f%%', shadow=True,
startangle=140)
```

plt.title('Monthly Expense Distribution')

plt.axis('equal')

plt.show()

Tips for Successful Data Visualization Projects

- **Define Clear Objectives**: Know what you want to achieve with your visualization.

- **Understand Your Audience**: Tailor your visuals to the knowledge level and interests of your audience.

- **Choose the Right Visualization Type**: Match the data and insights you want to convey with the appropriate chart type.

- **Maintain Clarity and Simplicity**: Avoid clutter; focus on making your visualization easy to interpret.

- **Iterate and Refine**: Continuously improve your visualizations based on feedback and new insights.

Exercise: Real-World Data Visualization Projects

1. **Choose a Project Topic**:

o Select a topic that interests you, such as sports, academics, personal habits, or finances.

2. **Collect and Prepare Data**:

    o Gather relevant data from reliable sources or create your own datasets.

    o Clean and organize the data using Pandas.

3. **Create Visualizations**:

    o Use Matplotlib to create at least two different types of charts representing different aspects of your data.

    o Use Plotly to build an interactive chart that allows deeper exploration.

4. **Analyze and Present Findings**:

    o Interpret the visualizations to draw meaningful conclusions.

    o Present your findings through a report, presentation, or interactive dashboard.

Example Project Idea:

Analyzing Your Weekly Gaming Hours and Performance.

- **Data Collection**:

    o Track hours spent gaming each day for eight weeks.

- Record performance metrics like levels achieved, scores, or achievements.

- **Data Preparation**:

  - Organize data into a CSV file with columns: Date, Hours Played, Level Achieved.

- **Visualization**:

  - Create a line chart showing hours played over time.

  - Develop a scatter plot to explore the relationship between hours played and levels achieved.

  - Build an interactive dashboard with Plotly to filter data by weeks and view detailed metrics.

- **Analysis**:

  - Determine if there's a correlation between gaming hours and performance.

  - Identify peak gaming periods and their impact on achievements.

Chapter 7: Exploring Advanced Topics

Welcome to **Chapter 7: Exploring Advanced Topics**! As you progress in your Python programming journey, it's essential to delve into more sophisticated concepts and tools that expand the capabilities of your applications. This chapter introduces you to **Object-Oriented Programming (OOP), Web Development with Flask, Machine Learning with Scikit-Learn**, and **Working with APIs and Web Services**. These advanced topics will empower you to build complex, efficient, and intelligent applications. Let's dive in!

7.1 Object-Oriented Programming Basics

What is Object-Oriented Programming (OOP)?

Object-Oriented Programming (OOP) is a programming paradigm that organizes software design around **objects** rather than functions and logic. An object can be defined as a data structure that contains data, in the form of fields (attributes or properties), and code, in the form of procedures (methods).

Key Concepts of OOP

1. **Classes and Objects**

2. **Attributes and Methods**

3. **Inheritance**

4. **Polymorphism**

5. **Encapsulation**

7.1.1 Classes and Objects

- **Class**: A blueprint for creating objects. It defines a set of attributes and methods that the created objects will have.

- **Object**: An instance of a class. It represents a specific entity with its own unique attributes.

Example: Defining a Simple Class

python

```python
class Dog:
    def __init__(self, name, age):
        self.name = name  # Attribute
        self.age = age    # Attribute

    def bark(self):       # Method
        print(f"{self.name} says woof!")
```

Explanation:

- __init__: The constructor method that initializes the object's attributes.

- self: Refers to the instance of the class.

Creating and Using Objects

python

```python
# Create an object of the Dog class
my_dog = Dog("Buddy", 3)

# Access attributes
print(my_dog.name)  # Output: Buddy
print(my_dog.age)   # Output: 3

# Call methods
my_dog.bark()      # Output: Buddy says woof!
```

7.1.2 Attributes and Methods

- **Attributes**: Variables that hold data specific to an object.

- **Methods**: Functions defined within a class that describe the behaviors of the objects.

Example: Extending the Dog Class

python

```python
class Dog:
    def __init__(self, name, age, breed):
        self.name = name
        self.age = age
        self.breed = breed

    def bark(self):
        print(f"{self.name} says woof!")

    def get_info(self):
        return f"{self.name} is a {self.age}-year-old {self.breed}."
```
python

```python
# Create an object
my_dog = Dog("Max", 5, "Labrador")

# Call methods
my_dog.bark()          # Output: Max says woof!
print(my_dog.get_info()) # Output: Max is a 5-year-old Labrador.
```

7.1.3 Inheritance

Inheritance allows a class (child class) to inherit attributes and methods from another class (parent class). This promotes code reusability and establishes a hierarchical relationship between classes.

Example: Parent and Child Classes

python

```python
class Animal:
    def __init__(self, name):
        self.name = name

    def eat(self):
        print(f"{self.name} is eating.")

class Cat(Animal):
    def meow(self):
        print(f"{self.name} says meow!")
```

python

```python
# Create an object of the Cat class
my_cat = Cat("Whiskers")

# Call inherited method
```

```python
my_cat.eat()     # Output: Whiskers is eating.


# Call Cat-specific method

my_cat.meow()    # Output: Whiskers says meow!
```

7.1.4 Polymorphism

Polymorphism allows objects of different classes to be treated as objects of a common superclass. It enables a single interface to represent different underlying forms (data types).

Example: Polymorphism with Animals

python

```python
class Dog(Animal):
    def make_sound(self):
        print(f"{self.name} says woof!")


class Cat(Animal):
    def make_sound(self):
        print(f"{self.name} says meow!")


def animal_sound(animal):
    animal.make_sound()
```

```python
# Create objects
dog = Dog("Buddy")
cat = Cat("Whiskers")

# Use polymorphism
animal_sound(dog)  # Output: Buddy says woof!
animal_sound(cat)  # Output: Whiskers says meow!
```

7.1.5 Encapsulation

Encapsulation is the bundling of data (attributes) and methods that operate on that data within a single unit (class). It restricts direct access to some of an object's components, which is a means of preventing accidental interference and misuse.

Example: Encapsulating Attributes

python

```python
class BankAccount:
    def __init__(self, balance):
        self.__balance = balance  # Private attribute

    def deposit(self, amount):
        self.__balance += amount
        print(f"Deposited ${amount}. New balance: ${self.__balance}")
```

```python
    def withdraw(self, amount):
        if amount <= self.__balance:
            self.__balance -= amount
            print(f"Withdrew ${amount}. New balance: ${self.__balance}")
        else:
            print("Insufficient funds.")

    def get_balance(self):
        return self.__balance
```
python

```python
# Create a BankAccount object
account = BankAccount(1000)


# Access methods
account.deposit(500)      # Output: Deposited $500. New balance: $1500

account.withdraw(200)     # Output: Withdrew $200. New balance: $1300

print(account.get_balance())  # Output: 1300
```

Attempt to access the private attribute

```python
print(account.__balance)   # AttributeError
```

Note: The double underscore (__) before balance makes it a private attribute, preventing direct access from outside the class.

7.1.6 Example: Simple OOP Program

Let's build a simple program that models a library system with books and members.

python


```python
class Book:
    def __init__(self, title, author):
        self.title = title
        self.author = author
        self.is_checked_out = False

    def check_out(self):
        if not self.is_checked_out:
            self.is_checked_out = True
            print(f"'{self.title}' has been checked out.")
        else:
            print(f"'{self.title}' is already checked out.")
```

```python
    def return_book(self):
        if self.is_checked_out:
            self.is_checked_out = False
            print(f"'{self.title}' has been returned.")
        else:
            print(f"'{self.title}' was not checked out.")


class Member:
    def __init__(self, name):
        self.name = name
        self.books_checked_out = []

    def borrow_book(self, book):
        if not book.is_checked_out:
            book.check_out()
            self.books_checked_out.append(book)
            print(f"{self.name} borrowed '{book.title}'.")
        else:
            print(f"Cannot borrow '{book.title}'. It is already
checked out.")

    def return_book(self, book):
```

```python
        if book in self.books_checked_out:
            book.return_book()
            self.books_checked_out.remove(book)
            print(f"{self.name} returned '{book.title}'.")
        else:
            print(f"{self.name} does not have '{book.title}'
checked out.")
```

python

```python
# Create books
book1 = Book("1984", "George Orwell")
book2 = Book("To Kill a Mockingbird", "Harper Lee")

# Create a member
member = Member("Alice")

# Member borrows a book
member.borrow_book(book1)
# Output:
# '1984' has been checked out.
# Alice borrowed '1984'.
```

```
# Attempt to borrow the same book again
member.borrow_book(book1)
# Output:
# '1984' is already checked out.
# Cannot borrow '1984'. It is already checked out.


# Member returns the book
member.return_book(book1)
# Output:
# '1984' has been returned.
# Alice returned '1984'.
```

Exercises

1. **Define a Class**:
    - Create a Car class with attributes make, model, and year.
    - Include methods to start_engine and stop_engine.

2. **Inheritance Practice**:
    - Define a Vehicle class with attributes make and model.
    - Create a Motorcycle class that inherits from Vehicle and adds an attribute engine_type.

3. **Encapsulation Challenge**:

- Implement a Student class with a private attribute __grades (a list).

- Provide methods to add_grade, get_average, and remove_grade.

7.2 Introduction to Web Development with Flask

What is Flask?

Flask is a lightweight and flexible web framework for Python. It is designed to make getting started quick and easy, with the ability to scale up to complex applications. Flask provides the tools, libraries, and technologies to build a web application.

Why Choose Flask?

- **Minimalistic**: Flask provides the essentials without enforcing a specific project structure.

- **Extensible**: Easily integrate with extensions for added functionality (e.g., database integration, form validation).

- **Pythonic**: Emphasizes simplicity and readability, adhering to Python's philosophy.

- **Large Community**: Extensive documentation and a supportive community make learning and troubleshooting easier.

Installing Flask

To install Flask, use pip:

bash

```
pip install Flask
```

Creating a Basic Flask Application

Let's create a simple "Hello, World!" web application using Flask.

Step-by-Step Guide

1. **Create a New Python File**:

   o Name it app.py.

2. **Write the Basic Flask Code**:

python

```python
from flask import Flask


# Initialize the Flask application
app = Flask(__name__)


# Define a route for the home page
@app.route('/')
def home():
    return "Hello, World!"
```

```python
# Run the application
if __name__ == '__main__':
    app.run(debug=True)
```

3. **Run the Application**:
   - Open your terminal or command prompt.
   - Navigate to the directory containing app.py.
   - Run the script:

bash

```bash
python app.py
```

   - You should see output indicating that the server is running, typically on http://127.0.0.1:5000/.

4. **View in Browser**:
   - Open your web browser.
   - Navigate to http://127.0.0.1:5000/.
   - You should see the message "Hello, World!".

Flask Routes and Views

Routes determine the URL patterns that trigger specific functions (**views**) in your application.

Example: Adding Multiple Routes

python

```python
from flask import Flask

app = Flask(__name__)

@app.route('/')
def home():
    return "Welcome to the Home Page!"

@app.route('/about')
def about():
    return "This is the About Page."

@app.route('/contact')
def contact():
    return "Contact us at contact@example.com."

if __name__ == '__main__':
    app.run(debug=True)
```

Explanation:

- Each @app.route() decorator defines a new URL route.

- Visiting /about will display "This is the About Page."

Using Templates with Flask

To create dynamic and reusable HTML pages, Flask uses the **Jinja2** templating engine.

Example: Rendering HTML Templates

1. **Project Structure**:

bash

```
/your_project
  /templates
    home.html
    about.html
  app.py
```

2. **Create home.html**:

html

```
<!DOCTYPE html>
<html>
<head>
  <title>Home Page</title>
```

```
</head>
<body>
    <h1>Welcome to the Home Page!</h1>
    <p>This is a simple Flask application.</p>
    <a href="/about">About</a>
</body>
</html>
```

3. **Create about.html**:

html

```
<!DOCTYPE html>
<html>
<head>
    <title>About Page</title>
</head>
<body>
    <h1>About This Application</h1>
    <p>This application is built using Flask.</p>
    <a href="/">Home</a>
</body>
</html>
```

4. **Update app.py to Use Templates**:

```python
from flask import Flask, render_template

app = Flask(__name__)

@app.route('/')
def home():
    return render_template('home.html')  # Render home.html

@app.route('/about')
def about():
    return render_template('about.html')  # Render about.html

if __name__ == '__main__':
    app.run(debug=True)
```

Explanation:

- **render_template()**: Renders an HTML template from the templates folder.
- Organizing templates allows for cleaner code and easier maintenance.

Passing Data to Templates

You can pass variables from your Flask routes to your HTML templates to create dynamic content.

Example: Dynamic Content with Variables

1. **Update home.html**:

html

```html
<!DOCTYPE html>
<html>
<head>
  <title>Home Page</title>
</head>
<body>
  <h1>Welcome, {{ username }}!</h1>
  <p>You have {{ notifications }} new notifications.</p>
  <a href="/about">About</a>
</body>
</html>
```

2. **Update app.py to Pass Variables**:

python

```python
from flask import Flask, render_template
```

```python
app = Flask(__name__)

@app.route('/')
def home():
    user = {
        'username': 'Alice',
        'notifications': 5
    }
    return render_template('home.html',
username=user['username'],
notifications=user['notifications'])


@app.route('/about')
def about():
    return render_template('about.html')


if __name__ == '__main__':
    app.run(debug=True)
```

Explanation:

- Variables username and notifications are passed to the template and rendered dynamically.

Example: Simple Web Application with Flask

Let's build a simple web application that greets users based on their input.

1. **Project Structure**:

bash

```
/flask_app

    /templates

        form.html

        greeting.html

    app.py
```

2. **Create form.html**:

html

```
<!DOCTYPE html>

<html>

<head>

    <title>Greeting Form</title>

</head>

<body>

    <h1>Enter Your Name</h1>

    <form action="/greet" method="post">
```

```
    <input type="text" name="username"
placeholder="Your Name" required>
    <button type="submit">Greet</button>
  </form>
</body>
</html>
```

3. **Create greeting.html**:

html

```
<!DOCTYPE html>
<html>
<head>
  <title>Greeting</title>
</head>
<body>
  <h1>Hello, {{ username }}!</h1>
  <a href="/">Back to Home</a>
</body>
</html>
```

4. **Write app.py**:

python

```python
from flask import Flask, render_template, request

app = Flask(__name__)

@app.route('/')
def form():
    return render_template('form.html')

@app.route('/greet', methods=['POST'])
def greet():
    username = request.form['username']
    return render_template('greeting.html',
username=username)

if __name__ == '__main__':
    app.run(debug=True)
```

5. **Run the Application**:
   o Execute app.py.
   o Navigate to http://127.0.0.1:5000/ in your browser.
   o Enter your name and submit the form to see the personalized greeting.

Exercises

1. **Create a Personal Portfolio Page**:
   - Design a simple portfolio website with pages like Home, Projects, and Contact.
   - Use templates to organize different sections.

2. **Build a To-Do List Web App**:
   - Allow users to add, view, and delete tasks.
   - Use Flask to handle routes and data management.

3. **Develop a Blog Platform**:
   - Implement functionality to create, read, update, and delete blog posts.
   - Incorporate user authentication for managing posts.

7.3 Basics of Machine Learning with Scikit-Learn

What is Machine Learning?

Machine Learning (ML) is a subset of artificial intelligence that enables computers to learn from data and make decisions or predictions without being explicitly programmed. ML algorithms build mathematical models based on sample data to make predictions or decisions.

Why Use Scikit-Learn?

Scikit-Learn is a powerful and user-friendly Python library for machine learning. It provides simple and efficient tools for data mining and data analysis, built on NumPy, SciPy, and matplotlib.

Installing Scikit-Learn

To install Scikit-Learn, use pip:

bash

```
pip install scikit-learn
```

Key Features of Scikit-Learn

- **Classification**: Identifying which category an object belongs to.

- **Regression**: Predicting a continuous-valued attribute.

- **Clustering**: Grouping a set of objects in such a way that objects in the same group are more similar.

- **Dimensionality Reduction**: Reducing the number of random variables.

- **Model Selection**: Comparing, validating, and choosing parameters and models.

- **Preprocessing**: Feature extraction and normalization.

Example: Predicting Iris Species

The Iris dataset is a classic dataset in machine learning, used for classification tasks. It contains measurements of iris flowers from three different species.

Step-by-Step Guide

    1. **Import Libraries**

python

```python
import matplotlib.pyplot as plt
from sklearn import datasets
from sklearn.model_selection import train_test_split
from sklearn.neighbors import KNeighborsClassifier
from sklearn.metrics import accuracy_score
```

    2. **Load the Dataset**

python

```python
# Load Iris dataset
iris = datasets.load_iris()
X = iris.data     # Features
y = iris.target   # Labels
```

    3. **Visualize the Data**

python

```python
# Scatter plot of the first two features
plt.scatter(X[:, 0], X[:, 1], c=y, cmap='viridis')
plt.xlabel(iris.feature_names[0])
plt.ylabel(iris.feature_names[1])
plt.title('Iris Dataset')
plt.show()
```

4. **Split the Dataset**

python

```python
# Split into training and testing sets (80% train, 20% test)
X_train, X_test, y_train, y_test = train_test_split(X, y, test_size=0.2, random_state=42)
```

5. **Train the Model**

python

```python
# Initialize KNN classifier with k=3
knn = KNeighborsClassifier(n_neighbors=3)
knn.fit(X_train, y_train)
```

6. **Make Predictions**

python

```python
# Predict the labels for the test set
```

```
y_pred = knn.predict(X_test)
```

7. **Evaluate the Model**

python

```
# Calculate accuracy
accuracy = accuracy_score(y_test, y_pred)
print(f"Accuracy: {accuracy * 100:.2f}%")
```

Output:

makefile

Accuracy: 100.00%

Explanation:

- The K-Nearest Neighbors (KNN) classifier achieved 100% accuracy on the test set.

Example: Logistic Regression for Binary Classification

Let's build a simple logistic regression model to classify whether a person has diabetes based on certain health metrics.

Step-by-Step Guide

1. **Import Libraries**

python

```python
import pandas as pd

import matplotlib.pyplot as plt

from sklearn.model_selection import train_test_split

from sklearn.linear_model import LogisticRegression

from sklearn.metrics import accuracy_score, confusion_matrix
```

2. Load the Dataset

We'll use the **Pima Indians Diabetes Dataset**, available from the UCI Machine Learning Repository.

python

```python
# Load dataset
url = "https://raw.githubusercontent.com/plotly/datasets/master/diabetes.csv"

df = pd.read_csv(url)


# Display first few rows
print(df.head())
```

3. Explore the Data

python

```python
# Summary statistics
```

```
print(df.describe())
```

```
# Check for missing values
print(df.isnull().sum())
```

4. **Prepare the Data**

python

```
# Features and target
X = df.drop('Outcome', axis=1)
y = df['Outcome']
```

```
# Split into training and testing sets (70% train, 30% test)
X_train, X_test, y_train, y_test = train_test_split(X, y, test_size=0.3, random_state=42)
```

5. **Train the Model**

python

```
# Initialize Logistic Regression model
model = LogisticRegression(max_iter=1000)
model.fit(X_train, y_train)
```

6. **Make Predictions**

python

```python
# Predict on the test set
y_pred = model.predict(X_test)
```

7. **Evaluate the Model**

python

```python
# Calculate accuracy
accuracy = accuracy_score(y_test, y_pred)
print(f"Accuracy: {accuracy * 100:.2f}%")
```

```python
# Confusion Matrix
cm = confusion_matrix(y_test, y_pred)
print("Confusion Matrix:")
print(cm)
```

Output:

lua

```
Accuracy: 77.78%
Confusion Matrix:
[[106  17]
 [ 34  43]]
```

Explanation:

- The model achieved an accuracy of approximately 77.78%.

- The confusion matrix shows true positives, true negatives, false positives, and false negatives.

Exercises

1. **Build a Decision Tree Classifier**:

   o Use the Iris dataset to build a decision tree classifier.

   o Visualize the decision tree using plot_tree from sklearn.tree.

2. **Implement a K-Means Clustering Model**:

   o Apply K-Means clustering on the Iris dataset.

   o Determine the optimal number of clusters using the Elbow Method.

3. **Evaluate Multiple Models**:

   o Compare the performance of different classifiers (e.g., KNN, Logistic Regression, Decision Trees) on the Pima Indians Diabetes Dataset.

   o Analyze which model performs best and why.

7.4 Working with APIs and Web Services

What are APIs?

APIs (Application Programming Interfaces) are sets of rules and protocols that allow different software applications to communicate with each other. They enable the integration of various services, data sources, and functionalities into your applications.

Types of APIs

1. **REST (Representational State Transfer)**: Uses standard HTTP methods and is stateless.

2. **SOAP (Simple Object Access Protocol)**: A protocol for exchanging structured information using XML.

3. **GraphQL**: A query language for APIs that allows clients to request specific data.

Why Use APIs?

- **Access External Data**: Retrieve data from third-party services (e.g., weather data, financial data).

- **Extend Functionality**: Incorporate features like authentication, payment processing, or messaging.

- **Integrate Services**: Connect different applications and automate workflows.

Working with RESTful APIs in Python

We'll use the **Requests** library to interact with RESTful APIs.

Installing Requests

To install the Requests library, use pip:

bash

```
pip install requests
```

Making HTTP Requests with Requests

The primary methods are GET, POST, PUT, DELETE, etc.

Example: GET Request

python

```
import requests

# API endpoint
url = "https://api.github.com/repos/python/cpython"

# Make a GET request
response = requests.get(url)

# Check status code
```

```python
print(response.status_code)  # Output: 200

# Parse JSON data
data = response.json()
print(data['full_name'])  # Output: python/cpython
```

Example: POST Request

python

```python
import requests

# API endpoint for creating a repository (Note:
Requires authentication)
url = "https://api.github.com/user/repos"
headers = {
    'Authorization': 'token YOUR_GITHUB_TOKEN'
}
payload = {
    'name': 'new-repo',
    'description': 'A new repository created via API',
    'private': False
}
```

```python
# Make a POST request
response = requests.post(url, json=payload,
headers=headers)


# Check response
print(response.status_code)  # Output: 201 (Created)
or other status codes
```

Note: Replace YOUR_GITHUB_TOKEN with a valid GitHub personal access token.

Parsing JSON Data

APIs often return data in JSON format, which can be easily parsed in Python.

Example: Accessing Nested JSON Data

python

```python
import requests


# API endpoint
url = "https://api.github.com/repos/python/cpython"


# Make a GET request
response = requests.get(url)
data = response.json()
```

```python
# Access nested data
owner = data['owner']['login']
stars = data['stargazers_count']

print(f"Repository Owner: {owner}")
print(f"Stars: {stars}")
```

Creating a Simple API with Flask

Flask can also be used to create your own APIs, allowing other applications to interact with your services.

Example: Building a Basic API

1. **Create a New Python File**:

   o Name it api_app.py.

2. **Write the Flask API Code**:

python

```python
from flask import Flask, jsonify, request

app = Flask(__name__)

# Sample data
books = [
```

```python
    {'id': 1, 'title': '1984', 'author': 'George Orwell'},
    {'id': 2, 'title': 'To Kill a Mockingbird', 'author':
'Harper Lee'}
]


@app.route('/api/books', methods=['GET'])
def get_books():
    return jsonify({'books': books})


@app.route('/api/books/<int:book_id>',
methods=['GET'])
def get_book(book_id):
    book = next((b for b in books if b['id'] == book_id),
None)
    if book:
        return jsonify({'book': book})
    else:
        return jsonify({'message': 'Book not found'}), 404


@app.route('/api/books', methods=['POST'])
def add_book():
    new_book = request.get_json()
    books.append(new_book)
```

```python
    return jsonify({'message': 'Book added
successfully'}), 201


if __name__ == '__main__':

    app.run(debug=True)
```

3. **Run the API Application**:

    o Execute api_app.py.

    o The API will be available at
      http://127.0.0.1:5000/api/books.

4. **Interact with the API**:

- **GET All Books**:

bash

```bash
curl http://127.0.0.1:5000/api/books
```

- **GET a Specific Book**:

bash

```bash
curl http://127.0.0.1:5000/api/books/1
```

- **POST a New Book**:

bash

```
curl -X POST -H "Content-Type: application/json" -d
'{"id":3, "title":"The Great Gatsby", "author":"F. Scott
Fitzgerald"}' http://127.0.0.1:5000/api/books
```

Exercises

1. **Consume a Public API**:

   o Use the OpenWeatherMap API to fetch
      and display current weather data for a
      specified city.

   o Display temperature, humidity, and
      weather conditions.

2. **Build a Simple RESTful API**:

   o Create an API for managing a list of
      students with operations to add,
      retrieve, update, and delete student
      records.

3. **Integrate API Data into a Flask Application**:

   o Build a Flask web app that fetches data
      from a public API and displays it to the
      user in a formatted manner.

4. **Error Handling in API Requests**:

   o Implement robust error handling for API
      requests, managing scenarios like
      invalid endpoints, timeouts, and
      malformed data.

Chapter 8: Real-World Applications and Projects

Welcome to **Chapter 8: Real-World Applications and Projects**! Applying your Python skills to real-world scenarios not only reinforces your learning but also showcases your abilities to solve practical problems. In this chapter, you'll embark on four comprehensive projects:

1. **Data Analysis Project: Exploring a Dataset**

2. **Game Development Project: Creating Your Own Game**

3. **Web Application Project: Building a Simple Website**

4. **Machine Learning Project: Predicting Outcomes**

Each project is designed to integrate various Python concepts and libraries you've learned, providing hands-on experience that bridges the gap between theory and practice. Let's dive into these exciting projects!

8.1 Data Analysis Project: Exploring a Dataset

Data analysis is a critical skill in today's data-driven world. By exploring and interpreting datasets, you can uncover valuable insights, inform decision-making, and present findings effectively.

Project Overview

Objective: Analyze a publicly available dataset to uncover trends, patterns, and insights.

Tools and Libraries:

- **Pandas**: For data manipulation and analysis.
- **Matplotlib/Seaborn**: For data visualization.
- **Jupyter Notebook**: For an interactive coding environment (optional but recommended).

Step-by-Step Guide

Step 1: Choose a Dataset

Select a dataset that interests you. Some popular sources include:

- Kaggle Datasets
- UCI Machine Learning Repository
- Data.gov

*For this project, we'll use the **Titanic Dataset** from Kaggle, which contains information about the passengers aboard the Titanic.*

Step 2: Set Up Your Environment

Ensure you have the necessary libraries installed. You can install them using pip:

bash

```
pip install pandas matplotlib seaborn jupyter
```

Step 3: Load the Dataset

python

```
import pandas as pd


# Load the Titanic dataset
url = 'https://raw.githubusercontent.com/datasciencedojo/datasets/master/titanic.csv'

titanic_df = pd.read_csv(url)


# Display the first five rows
print(titanic_df.head())
```

Step 4: Understand the Data

Explore the dataset to understand its structure, missing values, and data types.

python

```python
# Get basic information
print(titanic_df.info())
```

```python
# Summary statistics
print(titanic_df.describe())
```

```python
# Check for missing values
print(titanic_df.isnull().sum())
```

Step 5: Data Cleaning

Handle missing values and correct data types as necessary.

python

```python
# Fill missing 'Age' values with the median age
titanic_df['Age'].fillna(titanic_df['Age'].median(), inplace=True)
```

```python
# Drop rows with missing 'Embarked' values
titanic_df.dropna(subset=['Embarked'], inplace=True)
```

```python
# Verify no missing values remain
print(titanic_df.isnull().sum())
```

Step 6: Exploratory Data Analysis (EDA)

Conduct EDA to uncover patterns and relationships within the data.

Example Analyses:

1. **Survival Rate by Gender**

python

```
import matplotlib.pyplot as plt
import seaborn as sns

# Set the style
sns.set(style="darkgrid")

# Calculate survival rate by gender
gender_survival =
titanic_df.groupby('Sex')['Survived'].mean()

# Plot
gender_survival.plot(kind='bar', color=['skyblue',
'salmon'])
plt.title('Survival Rate by Gender')
plt.xlabel('Gender')
plt.ylabel('Survival Rate')
```

```
plt.ylim(0, 1)

plt.show()
```

2. Age Distribution of Passengers

python

```
plt.figure(figsize=(10,6))

sns.histplot(titanic_df['Age'], bins=30, kde=True,
color='green')

plt.title('Age Distribution of Titanic Passengers')

plt.xlabel('Age')

plt.ylabel('Frequency')

plt.show()
```

3. Survival Rate by Class

python

```
# Calculate survival rate by passenger class

class_survival =
titanic_df.groupby('Pclass')['Survived'].mean()


# Plot

class_survival.plot(kind='bar', color='purple')

plt.title('Survival Rate by Passenger Class')

plt.xlabel('Passenger Class')
```

```python
plt.ylabel('Survival Rate')
```

```python
plt.ylim(0, 1)
```

```python
plt.show()
```

Step 7: Advanced Visualization

Create more insightful visualizations to present your findings.

Example: Heatmap of Correlations

python

```python
plt.figure(figsize=(12,8))
```

```python
correlation_matrix = titanic_df.corr()
```

```python
sns.heatmap(correlation_matrix, annot=True, cmap='coolwarm', linewidths=0.5)
```

```python
plt.title('Correlation Heatmap of Titanic Dataset')
```

```python
plt.show()
```

Step 8: Draw Conclusions

Based on your analysis, summarize the key insights. For example:

- Females had a higher survival rate compared to males.

- Passengers in higher classes had better survival rates.

- Age showed a mild correlation with survival, indicating that younger passengers had slightly higher survival chances.

Step 9: Document Your Findings

Create a report or presentation summarizing your analysis, visualizations, and conclusions. Using Jupyter Notebook can be advantageous as it allows integrating code, visualizations, and markdown explanations seamlessly.

Example Project Structure

bash

```
/data_analysis_project

    /notebooks

        titanic_analysis.ipynb

    /data

        titanic.csv

    README.md
```

Exercise

1. **Choose a Different Dataset**:

   o Select another dataset of your choice and repeat the data analysis steps.

   o Example Datasets: Iris Dataset, COVID-19 Data

2. **Perform EDA**:

- Identify trends, patterns, and correlations within the new dataset.

- Create at least three different visualizations to support your findings.

3. **Present Your Analysis**:

- Compile your code, visualizations, and insights into a comprehensive report or a Jupyter Notebook.

8.2 Game Development Project: Creating Your Own Game

Game development is an exciting way to apply your programming skills creatively. Python offers libraries like **Pygame** that simplify the process of building games.

Project Overview

Objective: Develop a simple 2D game using Pygame.

Tools and Libraries:

- **Pygame**: A set of Python modules designed for writing video games.

- **Python**: Programming language.

Step-by-Step Guide

Step 1: Install Pygame

Install Pygame using pip:

```bash
pip install pygame
```

Step 2: Set Up Your Project Structure

Organize your project files:

```bash
/game_project
    /assets
        player.png
        enemy.png
        background.png
    game.py
```

Ensure you have appropriate asset images (player, enemy, background) placed in the assets folder.

Step 3: Initialize Pygame and Create the Game Window

```python
import pygame
import sys


# Initialize Pygame
```

```python
pygame.init()

# Set up display
SCREEN_WIDTH = 800
SCREEN_HEIGHT = 600
screen = pygame.display.set_mode((SCREEN_WIDTH, SCREEN_HEIGHT))
pygame.display.set_caption("My First Game")

# Set up the clock for frame rate
clock = pygame.time.Clock()

# Game loop
running = True
while running:
    # Handle events
    for event in pygame.event.get():
        if event.type == pygame.QUIT:
            running = False

    # Fill the screen with a color
    screen.fill((0, 0, 0))  # Black background
```

```python
    # Update the display
    pygame.display.flip()


    # Cap the frame rate at 60 FPS
    clock.tick(60)


# Quit Pygame
pygame.quit()
sys.exit()
```

Explanation:

- **pygame.init()**: Initializes all Pygame modules.
- **pygame.display.set_mode()**: Sets up the game window.
- **Game Loop**: Keeps the game running until the user quits.

Step 4: Add a Player Character

python

```python
import pygame
import sys


# Initialize Pygame
```

```python
pygame.init()

# Set up display
SCREEN_WIDTH = 800
SCREEN_HEIGHT = 600
screen = pygame.display.set_mode((SCREEN_WIDTH,
SCREEN_HEIGHT))
pygame.display.set_caption("My First Game")

# Set up the clock for frame rate
clock = pygame.time.Clock()

# Load player image
player_image =
pygame.image.load('assets/player.png').convert_alph
a()
player_rect = player_image.get_rect()
player_rect.center = (SCREEN_WIDTH//2,
SCREEN_HEIGHT - 50)

# Player speed
player_speed = 5
```

```python
# Game loop
running = True
while running:
    # Handle events
    for event in pygame.event.get():
        if event.type == pygame.QUIT:
            running = False

    # Handle key presses for movement
    keys = pygame.key.get_pressed()
    if keys[pygame.K_LEFT] and player_rect.left > 0:
        player_rect.x -= player_speed
    if keys[pygame.K_RIGHT] and player_rect.right < SCREEN_WIDTH:
        player_rect.x += player_speed

    # Fill the screen with a color
    screen.fill((0, 0, 0))  # Black background

    # Draw the player
    screen.blit(player_image, player_rect)
```

```python
# Update the display
pygame.display.flip()

# Cap the frame rate at 60 FPS
clock.tick(60)
```

```python
# Quit Pygame
pygame.quit()
sys.exit()
```

Explanation:

- **pygame.image.load()**: Loads the player image.
- **player_rect**: Defines the position and size of the player.
- **Keyboard Input**: Moves the player left or right based on key presses.

Step 5: Add Enemies

python

```python
import pygame
import sys
import random
```

```python
# Initialize Pygame
pygame.init()


# Set up display
SCREEN_WIDTH = 800

SCREEN_HEIGHT = 600

screen =
pygame.display.set_mode((SCREEN_WIDTH,
SCREEN_HEIGHT))

pygame.display.set_caption("My First Game")


# Set up the clock for frame rate
clock = pygame.time.Clock()


# Load images
player_image =
pygame.image.load('assets/player.png').convert_alph
a()

enemy_image =
pygame.image.load('assets/enemy.png').convert_alph
a()

background_image =
pygame.image.load('assets/background.png').convert
()
```

```python
# Player setup
player_rect = player_image.get_rect()
player_rect.center = (SCREEN_WIDTH//2,
SCREEN_HEIGHT - 50)
player_speed = 5


# Enemy setup
enemy_rect = enemy_image.get_rect()
enemy_rect.x = random.randint(0, SCREEN_WIDTH -
enemy_rect.width)
enemy_rect.y = -enemy_rect.height
enemy_speed = 3


# Game loop
running = True
while running:
    # Handle events
    for event in pygame.event.get():
        if event.type == pygame.QUIT:
            running = False


    # Handle key presses for movement
    keys = pygame.key.get_pressed()
```

```python
    if keys[pygame.K_LEFT] and player_rect.left > 0:
        player_rect.x -= player_speed
    if keys[pygame.K_RIGHT] and player_rect.right <
SCREEN_WIDTH:
        player_rect.x += player_speed


    # Move the enemy
    enemy_rect.y += enemy_speed
    if enemy_rect.y > SCREEN_HEIGHT:
        enemy_rect.x = random.randint(0,
SCREEN_WIDTH - enemy_rect.width)
        enemy_rect.y = -enemy_rect.height


    # Collision detection
    if player_rect.colliderect(enemy_rect):
        print("Collision Detected! Game Over.")
        running = False


    # Draw background
    screen.blit(background_image, (0, 0))


    # Draw the player and enemy
    screen.blit(player_image, player_rect)
```

```
    screen.blit(enemy_image, enemy_rect)

    # Update the display
    pygame.display.flip()

    # Cap the frame rate at 60 FPS
    clock.tick(60)

# Quit Pygame
pygame.quit()
sys.exit()
```

Explanation:

- **Enemy Movement**: Enemies move downward; when they exit the screen, they reset to the top at a random horizontal position.

- **Collision Detection**: Checks if the player collides with an enemy, ending the game if a collision occurs.

Step 6: Add Multiple Enemies and Game Mechanics

Enhance the game by adding multiple enemies, scoring, and increasing difficulty.

python

```python
import pygame
import sys
import random

# Initialize Pygame
pygame.init()

# Set up display
SCREEN_WIDTH = 800
SCREEN_HEIGHT = 600
screen = pygame.display.set_mode((SCREEN_WIDTH,
SCREEN_HEIGHT))
pygame.display.set_caption("My First Game")

# Set up the clock for frame rate
clock = pygame.time.Clock()

# Load images
player_image =
pygame.image.load('assets/player.png').convert_alph
a()
```

```python
enemy_image =
pygame.image.load('assets/enemy.png').convert_alph
a()

background_image =
pygame.image.load('assets/background.png').convert
()


# Player setup

player_rect = player_image.get_rect()

player_rect.center = (SCREEN_WIDTH//2,
SCREEN_HEIGHT - 50)

player_speed = 7


# Enemy setup

enemy_list = []

num_enemies = 5

enemy_speed = 3


for _ in range(num_enemies):

    enemy_rect = enemy_image.get_rect()

    enemy_rect.x = random.randint(0,
SCREEN_WIDTH - enemy_rect.width)

    enemy_rect.y = random.randint(-150, -
enemy_rect.height)
```

```python
    enemy_list.append(enemy_rect)

# Score setup
score = 0
font = pygame.font.SysFont(None, 36)

# Game loop
running = True
while running:
    # Handle events
    for event in pygame.event.get():
        if event.type == pygame.QUIT:
            running = False

    # Handle key presses for movement
    keys = pygame.key.get_pressed()
    if keys[pygame.K_LEFT] and player_rect.left > 0:
        player_rect.x -= player_speed
    if keys[pygame.K_RIGHT] and player_rect.right <
SCREEN_WIDTH:
        player_rect.x += player_speed
```

```python
    # Move enemies
    for enemy_rect in enemy_list:
        enemy_rect.y += enemy_speed
        if enemy_rect.y > SCREEN_HEIGHT:
            enemy_rect.x = random.randint(0,
SCREEN_WIDTH - enemy_rect.width)
            enemy_rect.y = random.randint(-150, -
enemy_rect.height)
            score += 1  # Increment score for avoiding an
enemy


    # Collision detection
    for enemy_rect in enemy_list:
        if player_rect.colliderect(enemy_rect):
            print(f"Collision Detected! Final Score:
{score}")
            running = False


    # Draw background
    screen.blit(background_image, (0, 0))


    # Draw the player and enemies
    screen.blit(player_image, player_rect)
```

```python
    for enemy_rect in enemy_list:

        screen.blit(enemy_image, enemy_rect)


    # Render the score

    score_text = font.render(f"Score: {score}", True,
(255, 255, 255))

    screen.blit(score_text, (10, 10))


    # Update the display

    pygame.display.flip()


    # Cap the frame rate at 60 FPS

    clock.tick(60)


# Quit Pygame

pygame.quit()

sys.exit()
```

Enhancements:

- **Multiple Enemies**: Adds five enemies moving independently.
- **Scoring System**: Increments the score each time an enemy is avoided.

- **Game Over Message**: Displays the final score upon collision.

Exercise

1. **Add Sound Effects**:

   - Incorporate background music and sound effects for actions like moving, collisions, and scoring.

   - Use pygame.mixer to handle audio.

2. **Implement Power-Ups**:

   - Add power-up items that grant the player temporary abilities (e.g., increased speed, invincibility).

   - Handle their appearance, effects, and duration.

3. **Enhance Graphics**:

   - Replace placeholder images with custom sprites.

   - Add animations for smoother movements and actions.

4. **Create a Main Menu**:

   - Design a start screen with options like "Play", "Instructions", and "Quit".

   - Navigate between different game states based on user input.

Recommended Resources

- **Pygame Documentation**:
  https://www.pygame.org/docs/

- **Pygame Tutorials**:

  - Official Pygame Tutorials

  - Real Python's Pygame Tutorial

- **Books**:

  - **"Making Games with Python & Pygame"** by Al Sweigart

8.3 Web Application Project: Building a Simple Website

Web development allows you to create dynamic websites and applications accessible to users worldwide. **Flask**, a lightweight Python web framework, simplifies the process of building web applications.

Project Overview

Objective: Develop a simple personal blog website where users can view posts.

Tools and Libraries:

- **Flask**: Web framework.

- **SQLite**: Lightweight database.

- **Jinja2**: Templating engine (included with Flask).

- **HTML/CSS**: For frontend design.

Step-by-Step Guide

Step 1: Set Up Your Environment

Ensure Flask is installed:

bash

pip install Flask

Step 2: Create the Project Structure

Organize your project files:

bash

```
/web_app_project
    /templates
        base.html
        home.html
        post.html
    /static
        /css
            styles.css
    app.py
    database.db
```

Step 3: Initialize the Database

We'll use SQLite for simplicity.

python

```
import sqlite3

# Connect to SQLite database (creates it if it doesn't
exist)
conn = sqlite3.connect('database.db')
c = conn.cursor()

# Create a table for blog posts
c.execute('''
    CREATE TABLE IF NOT EXISTS posts (
        id INTEGER PRIMARY KEY
AUTOINCREMENT,
        title TEXT NOT NULL,
        content TEXT NOT NULL
    )
''')

# Insert sample posts
c.execute('INSERT INTO posts (title, content)
VALUES (?, ?)',
```

```
        ('First Post', 'This is the content of the first
post.'))
c.execute('INSERT INTO posts (title, content)
VALUES (?, ?)',
        ('Second Post', 'This is the content of the
second post.'))


# Commit changes and close connection
conn.commit()
conn.close()
```

Run this script once to set up the database.

Step 4: Create Flask Routes and Views

python

```python
from flask import Flask, render_template
import sqlite3


app = Flask(__name__)


def get_db_connection():
    conn = sqlite3.connect('database.db')
    conn.row_factory = sqlite3.Row  # Enable dict-like
access
```

```python
    return conn

@app.route('/')
def home():
    conn = get_db_connection()
    posts = conn.execute('SELECT * FROM
posts').fetchall()
    conn.close()
    return render_template('home.html', posts=posts)


@app.route('/post/<int:post_id>')
def post(post_id):
    conn = get_db_connection()
    post = conn.execute('SELECT * FROM posts
WHERE id = ?', (post_id,)).fetchone()
    conn.close()
    if post is None:
        return "Post not found!", 404
    return render_template('post.html', post=post)


if __name__ == '__main__':
    app.run(debug=True)
```
Explanation:

- **get_db_connection()**: Establishes a connection to the SQLite database.

- **Home Route ('/')**: Displays all blog posts.

- **Post Route ('/post/<id>')**: Displays a specific post based on its ID.

Step 5: Create HTML Templates

1. **base.html**: Base template that other templates inherit from.

html

```html
<!DOCTYPE html>
<html>
<head>
    <title>My Blog</title>
    <link rel="stylesheet" href="{{ url_for('static', filename='css/styles.css') }}">
</head>
<body>
    <header>
        <h1><a href="/">My Blog</a></h1>
    </header>
    <main>
        {% block content %}{% endblock %}
```

```html
    </main>
    <footer>
        <p>&copy; 2024 My Blog</p>
    </footer>
</body>
</html>
```

2. **home.html**: Displays a list of blog posts.

html

```html
{% extends 'base.html' %}

{% block content %}
    <h2>All Posts</h2>
    <ul>
        {% for post in posts %}
            <li>
                <a href="{{ url_for('post', post_id=post['id']) }}">{{ post['title'] }}</a>
            </li>
        {% endfor %}
    </ul>
{% endblock %}
```

3. **post.html**: Displays the content of a single post.

html

```
{% extends 'base.html' %}

{% block content %}
    <h2>{{ post['title'] }}</h2>
    <p>{{ post['content'] }}</p>
    <a href="/">Back to Home</a>
{% endblock %}
```

Step 6: Add CSS for Styling

Create styles.css in /static/css/:

css

```
body {
    font-family: Arial, sans-serif;
    background-color: #f4f4f4;
    margin: 0;
    padding: 0;
}
```

```css
header {
    background-color: #35424a;
    color: #ffffff;
    padding: 20px 0;
    text-align: center;
}

header a {
    color: #ffffff;
    text-decoration: none;
}

main {
    padding: 20px;
}

h1, h2 {
    color: #333333;
}

ul {
    list-style-type: none;
```

```css
    padding: 0;
}

li {
    background-color: #ffffff;
    margin-bottom: 10px;
    padding: 10px;
    border-radius: 5px;
}

li a {
    text-decoration: none;
    color: #35424a;
    font-weight: bold;
}

footer {
    background-color: #35424a;
    color: #ffffff;
    text-align: center;
    padding: 10px 0;
    position: fixed;
```

```
    width: 100%;

    bottom: 0;

}
```

Explanation:

- Provides a clean and simple design for the blog website.
- Styles headers, links, lists, and the footer.

Step 7: Run the Application

Navigate to your project directory in the terminal and run:

bash

```
python app.py
```

Open your browser and go to http://127.0.0.1:5000/ to view your blog.

Exercise

1. **Add Functionality to Create New Posts**:
   - Implement a form where users can submit new blog posts.
   - Handle form submissions and update the database accordingly.

2. **Enhance the Design**:

- Improve the website's aesthetics using advanced CSS or frameworks like Bootstrap.
- Add images, navigation menus, and responsive design.

3. **Implement User Authentication**:
   - Allow users to register and log in to create or edit posts.
   - Secure routes to prevent unauthorized access.

4. **Add a Database ORM**:
   - Use **SQLAlchemy** to interact with the database more efficiently.
   - Replace raw SQL queries with ORM methods.

Recommended Resources

- **Flask Documentation**: https://flask.palletsprojects.com/
- **Flask Tutorials**:
  - Official Flask Tutorial
  - Real Python's Flask Tutorials
- **Books**:
  - **"Flask Web Development"** by Miguel Grinberg

8.4 Machine Learning Project: Predicting Outcomes

Machine Learning (ML) enables computers to learn from data and make predictions or decisions without being explicitly programmed. This project guides you through building a simple ML model to predict outcomes based on historical data.

Project Overview

Objective: Develop a machine learning model to predict whether a person has diabetes based on health metrics.

Tools and Libraries:

- **Pandas**: For data manipulation.

- **Scikit-Learn**: For building and evaluating ML models.

- **Matplotlib/Seaborn**: For data visualization.

Step-by-Step Guide

Step 1: Import Libraries

python

```
import pandas as pd

import matplotlib.pyplot as plt

import seaborn as sns

from sklearn.model_selection import train_test_split
```

```python
from sklearn.preprocessing import StandardScaler

from sklearn.linear_model import LogisticRegression

from sklearn.metrics import classification_report,
confusion_matrix, accuracy_score
```

Step 2: Load the Dataset

We'll use the **Pima Indians Diabetes Dataset** available from the UCI Machine Learning Repository.

python

```python
# Load dataset

url =
"https://raw.githubusercontent.com/plotly/datasets/ma
ster/diabetes.csv"

df = pd.read_csv(url)


# Display first five rows

print(df.head())
```

Step 3: Explore the Data

Understand the dataset's structure, statistics, and any potential issues.

python

```python
# Summary statistics
print(df.describe())
```

```
# Check for missing values

print(df.isnull().sum())


# Count of target classes

print(df['Outcome'].value_counts())
```

Note: In this dataset, 0 represents no diabetes, and 1 represents diabetes.

Step 4: Data Visualization

Visualize the relationships between features and the target variable.

Example: Correlation Heatmap

python

```
plt.figure(figsize=(10,8))

sns.heatmap(df.corr(), annot=True, cmap='coolwarm')

plt.title('Correlation Heatmap')

plt.show()
```

Example: Distribution of Age

python

```
plt.figure(figsize=(8,6))
```

```python
sns.histplot(df['Age'], bins=30, kde=True,
color='green')
```

```python
plt.title('Age Distribution')
```

```python
plt.xlabel('Age')
```

```python
plt.ylabel('Frequency')
```

```python
plt.show()
```

Step 5: Data Preprocessing

Prepare the data for modeling by handling missing values, encoding categorical variables, and scaling features.

python

```python
# Replace zeros with NaN for specific columns where zero is invalid

cols_with_zero = ['Glucose', 'BloodPressure',
'SkinThickness', 'Insulin', 'BMI']

df[cols_with_zero] = df[cols_with_zero].replace(0,
pd.NA)


# Fill NaN values with the median of each column

df.fillna(df.median(), inplace=True)


# Verify no missing values remain

print(df.isnull().sum())
```

```python
# Features and target
X = df.drop('Outcome', axis=1)
y = df['Outcome']
```

```python
# Split into training and testing sets (80% train, 20% test)
X_train, X_test, y_train, y_test = train_test_split(X, y, test_size=0.2, random_state=42)
```

```python
# Feature scaling
scaler = StandardScaler()
X_train = scaler.fit_transform(X_train)
X_test = scaler.transform(X_test)
```

Step 6: Train the Model

We'll use **Logistic Regression** for this binary classification task.

python

```python
# Initialize the model
model = LogisticRegression()
```

```python
# Train the model
```

```python
model.fit(X_train, y_train)
```

Step 7: Make Predictions

python

```python
# Predict on the test set
y_pred = model.predict(X_test)
```

Step 8: Evaluate the Model

Assess the performance of your model using various metrics.

python

```python
# Accuracy
accuracy = accuracy_score(y_test, y_pred)
print(f"Accuracy: {accuracy * 100:.2f}%")


# Classification Report
print("Classification Report:")
print(classification_report(y_test, y_pred))


# Confusion Matrix
conf_matrix = confusion_matrix(y_test, y_pred)
sns.heatmap(conf_matrix, annot=True, fmt='d', cmap='Blues')
```

```
plt.title('Confusion Matrix')
plt.xlabel('Predicted')
plt.ylabel('Actual')
plt.show()
```

Sample Output:

markdown

Accuracy: 77.78%

Classification Report:

	precision	recall	f1-score	support
0	0.85	0.80	0.82	35
1	0.78	0.83	0.80	41
accuracy			0.78	76
macro avg	0.82	0.82	0.81	76
weighted avg	0.81	0.78	0.80	76

Explanation:

- **Accuracy**: The model correctly predicted 77.78% of the cases.

- **Confusion Matrix**: Shows the number of true positives, true negatives, false positives, and false negatives.

- **Classification Report**: Provides precision, recall, and F1-score for each class.

Step 9: Improve the Model

Experiment with different algorithms or tweak hyperparameters to enhance performance.

Example: Using a Decision Tree Classifier

python

```python
from sklearn.tree import DecisionTreeClassifier


# Initialize the model
dt_model = DecisionTreeClassifier(random_state=42)


# Train the model
dt_model.fit(X_train, y_train)


# Predict
y_pred_dt = dt_model.predict(X_test)


# Evaluate
accuracy_dt = accuracy_score(y_test, y_pred_dt)
print(f"Decision Tree Accuracy: {accuracy_dt * 100:.2f}%")
```

```
print("Classification Report:")

print(classification_report(y_test, y_pred_dt))
```

Compare the accuracy and other metrics with the Logistic Regression model to determine which performs better.

Exercise

1. **Try a Different Algorithm**:

   - Implement a **Random Forest Classifier** and evaluate its performance.

   - Compare its results with Logistic Regression and Decision Tree models.

2. **Hyperparameter Tuning**:

   - Use **Grid Search** or **Randomized Search** to find the optimal hyperparameters for your chosen model.

   - Assess how tuning affects the model's performance.

3. **Feature Engineering**:

   - Create new features or modify existing ones to improve model accuracy.

   - For example, combine Glucose and BMI into a new feature that might better predict the outcome.

4. **Cross-Validation**:

- Implement **k-Fold Cross-Validation** to assess the model's robustness.

- Calculate average performance metrics across different folds.

Recommended Resources

- **Scikit-Learn Documentation**: https://scikit-learn.org/stable/documentation.html

- **Machine Learning Tutorials**:
  - Real Python's Machine Learning with Scikit-Learn

  - Kaggle's Intro to Machine Learning

- **Books**:
  - **"Hands-On Machine Learning with Scikit-Learn, Keras, and TensorFlow"** by Aurélien Géron

  - **"Python Machine Learning"** by Sebastian Raschk.

Chapter 9: Challenges and Solutions

Welcome to **Chapter 9: Challenges and Solutions**! As you delve deeper into Python programming, you'll inevitably encounter various challenges that test your understanding and problem-solving skills. This chapter is dedicated to equipping you with the knowledge and techniques to overcome common programming errors, master debugging, optimize your code for better performance, and adhere to best practices for writing clean and maintainable code. Let's explore these essential aspects to enhance your programming proficiency.

9.1 Common Programming Errors and How to Fix Them

Encountering errors is a natural part of the programming journey. Understanding common errors and knowing how to resolve them is crucial for efficient coding and development.

9.1.1 Syntax Errors

Syntax errors occur when Python cannot parse your code because it doesn't follow the correct syntax. These errors are detected before the program runs.

Example: Missing Colon

python

```
# Incorrect Code
if x > 5
    print("x is greater than 5")
```

Error Message:

arduino

```
  File "example.py", line 2
    if x > 5
            ^
SyntaxError: invalid syntax
```

Solution:

Ensure that all control structures (like if, for, while, etc.) end with a colon (:).

python

```
# Correct Code
```

```python
if x > 5:

    print("x is greater than 5")
```

9.1.2 Indentation Errors

Indentation errors arise when the code blocks are not properly indented. Python uses indentation to define the scope of loops, functions, classes, etc.

Example: Inconsistent Indentation

python

```python
def greet(name):
print(f"Hello, {name}!")
    print("Welcome to Python programming.")
```

Error Message:

arduino

```
  File "example.py", line 2
    print(f"Hello, {name}!")
    ^
IndentationError: expected an indented block after function definition on line 1
```

Solution:

Consistently indent your code blocks, typically using four spaces per indentation level.

```python
python
```

```python
def greet(name):
    print(f"Hello, {name}!")
    print("Welcome to Python programming.")
```

9.1.3 Name Errors

Name errors occur when you try to use a variable or function name that hasn't been defined.

Example: Undefined Variable

```python
python
```

```python
# Incorrect Code
print(message)
```

Error Message:

```csharp
csharp
```

```
NameError: name 'message' is not defined
```

Solution:

Ensure that all variables and functions are defined before use.

```python
python
```

```python
# Correct Code
```

```python
message = "Hello, World!"
print(message)
```

9.1.4 Type Errors

Type errors happen when an operation or function is applied to an object of inappropriate type.

Example: Adding String and Integer

python

```python
# Incorrect Code
age = "25"
new_age = age + 5
```

Error Message:

python

```python
TypeError: can only concatenate str (not "int") to str
```

Solution:

Ensure that operands are of compatible types. Convert types if necessary.

python

```python
# Correct Code
age = "25"
new_age = int(age) + 5
```

```
print(new_age)  # Output: 30
```

9.1.5 Index Errors

Index errors occur when you try to access an index that is out of range for a list or other indexable objects.

Example: Accessing Invalid List Index

python

```python
# Incorrect Code
fruits = ['apple', 'banana', 'cherry']
print(fruits[3])
```

Error Message:

sql

```
IndexError: list index out of range
```

Solution:

Ensure that the index exists within the bounds of the list. Use functions like len() to check the list size.

python

```python
# Correct Code
fruits = ['apple', 'banana', 'cherry']
index = 2
```

```python
if index < len(fruits):
    print(fruits[index])  # Output: cherry
else:
    print("Index out of range.")
```

9.1.6 Key Errors

Key errors happen when you try to access a key that doesn't exist in a dictionary.

Example: Accessing Non-existent Dictionary Key

python

```python
# Incorrect Code
student = {'name': 'Alice', 'age': 25}
print(student['grade'])
```

Error Message:

vbnet

```
KeyError: 'grade'
```

Solution:

Check if the key exists using methods like .get() or in keyword.

python

```python
# Correct Code
```

```python
student = {'name': 'Alice', 'age': 25}

grade = student.get('grade', 'Not Available')

print(grade)  # Output: Not Available
```

9.2 Debugging Techniques

Effective debugging is essential for identifying and resolving issues in your code. Here are several techniques and tools to enhance your debugging skills.

9.2.1 Print Statement Debugging

One of the simplest debugging methods is inserting print() statements to check the values of variables at different stages of your program.

Example:

python

```python
def calculate_total(items):

    total = 0

    for item in items:

        print(f"Adding {item} to total.")  # Debugging statement

        total += item
```

```
    print(f"Final total: {total}")        # Debugging
statement

    return total


calculate_total([10, 20, 30])
```

Output:

```
css
```

Adding 10 to total.

Adding 20 to total.

Adding 30 to total.

Final total: 60

Pros:

- Simple and quick to implement.

- Helps trace the flow of execution.

Cons:

- Can clutter the code with print statements.

- Not efficient for large or complex programs.

9.2.2 Using Assertions

Assertions are statements that check if a condition is True. If the condition is False, the program raises an AssertionError.

Example:

```python
python
```

```python
def divide(a, b):
    assert b != 0, "Division by zero is not allowed."
    return a / b


print(divide(10, 2))  # Output: 5.0
print(divide(10, 0))  # Raises AssertionError
```

Pros:

- Helps catch unexpected states.
- Clear error messages for failed conditions.

Cons:

- Assertions can be disabled with optimization flags, so they shouldn't replace proper error handling.

9.2.3 Using a Debugger

Python provides built-in debugging tools like pdb (Python Debugger) that allow you to step through your code, inspect variables, and evaluate expressions interactively.

Example: Using pdb

```python
python
```

```python
import pdb
```

```
def multiply(a, b):
    pdb.set_trace()  # Initiates the debugger
    result = a * b
    return result


print(multiply(5, 3))
```

How to Use:

1. Run the script.
2. The debugger will pause execution at pdb.set_trace().
3. Use commands like n (next), c (continue), p (print variable), and q (quit) to navigate.

Pros:

- Powerful tool for in-depth debugging.
- Allows real-time inspection and modification of variables.

Cons:

- Steeper learning curve compared to print statements.
- Can be time-consuming for simple errors.

9.2.4 Integrated Development Environment (IDE) Debuggers

Modern IDEs like **PyCharm**, **VS Code**, and **Eclipse with PyDev** offer advanced debugging features, including breakpoints, variable watches, and step-through execution.

Example: Debugging in VS Code

1. **Set Breakpoints**: Click next to the line numbers to set breakpoints.

2. **Start Debugging**: Press F5 or click the debug icon to start.

3. **Inspect Variables**: Hover over variables to see their current values.

4. **Step Through Code**: Use the debug toolbar to step into, over, or out of functions.

Pros:

- User-friendly interface.

- Advanced features like conditional breakpoints and call stacks.

- Seamless integration with code editors.

Cons:

- Requires familiarity with the IDE.

- May consume more system resources.

9.3 Optimizing Your Code

Writing efficient code is crucial for improving performance, reducing resource consumption, and enhancing scalability. Here are strategies to optimize your Python code.

9.3.1 Time Complexity Optimization

Time complexity refers to how the runtime of an algorithm increases with the size of the input. Optimizing time complexity can significantly speed up your programs.

Example: Optimizing a Loop

Inefficient Code: Checking for duplicates in a list using nested loops.

python

```python
def has_duplicates(lst):
    for i in range(len(lst)):
        for j in range(i + 1, len(lst)):
            if lst[i] == lst[j]:
                return True
    return False
```

Time Complexity: $O(n^2)$

Optimized Code: Using a set to track seen elements.

python

```python
def has_duplicates(lst):
    seen = set()
    for item in lst:
        if item in seen:
            return True
        seen.add(item)
    return False
```

Time Complexity: O(n)

9.3.2 Space Complexity Optimization

Space complexity deals with the amount of memory an algorithm uses relative to the input size.

Example: In-Place Operations

Inefficient Code: Creating a new list to store squared values.

python

```python
def square_numbers(lst):
    squared = []
    for num in lst:
        squared.append(num ** 2)
    return squared
```

Space Complexity: O(n)

Optimized Code: Modifying the list in place.

python

```python
def square_numbers(lst):
    for i in range(len(lst)):
        lst[i] = lst[i] ** 2
    return lst
```

Space Complexity: O(1)

9.3.3 Leveraging Built-in Functions and Libraries

Python's built-in functions and standard libraries are optimized for performance. Utilizing them can lead to more efficient code.

Example: Using List Comprehensions

Inefficient Code: Using a loop to create a list of squares.

python

```python
def get_squares(lst):
    squares = []
    for num in lst:
        squares.append(num ** 2)
    return squares
```

Optimized Code: Using list comprehensions.

python

```python
def get_squares(lst):
    return [num ** 2 for num in lst]
```

Pros:

- Faster execution.
- More concise and readable.

9.3.4 Profiling Your Code

Profiling helps identify bottlenecks in your code by measuring the time and memory consumption of different parts.

Example: Using cProfile

python

```python
import cProfile

def compute():
    total = 0
    for i in range(1000000):
        total += i
    return total

cProfile.run('compute()')
```

Output:

```sql
        4 function calls in 0.054 seconds

   Ordered by: standard name

   ncalls  tottime  percall  cumtime  percall filename:lineno(function)
        1    0.054    0.054    0.054    0.054 example.py:4(compute)
        1    0.000    0.000    0.054    0.054 {built-in method builtins.exec}
        1    0.000    0.000    0.000    0.000 {method 'disable' of '_lsprof.Profiler' objects}
```

Pros:

- Identifies slow functions and loops.
- Provides detailed statistics for optimization.

Cons:

- Adds overhead to execution time.
- Can be overwhelming for large codebases.

9.3.5 Parallel and Asynchronous Processing

Leveraging parallelism and asynchronous programming can significantly enhance performance, especially for I/O-bound and CPU-bound tasks.

Example: Using multiprocessing for Parallel Processing

python

```python
import multiprocessing


def square(num):
    return num ** 2


if __name__ == '__main__':
    numbers = [1, 2, 3, 4, 5]
    with multiprocessing.Pool() as pool:
        results = pool.map(square, numbers)
    print(results)  # Output: [1, 4, 9, 16, 25]
```

Pros:

- Utilizes multiple CPU cores.
- Reduces execution time for large datasets.

Cons:

- More complex to implement.

- Potential issues with shared resources and data synchronization.

9.4 Best Practices for Writing Clean Code

Writing clean, readable, and maintainable code is essential for collaboration, scalability, and long-term project success. Here are some best practices to follow.

9.4.1 Follow Naming Conventions

Consistent naming improves code readability and understanding.

- **Variables and Functions**: Use snake_case.

python

```python
def calculate_total():
    total_amount = 0
    return total_amount
```

- **Classes**: Use CamelCase.

python

```python
class DataProcessor:
    pass
```

- **Constants**: Use UPPER_SNAKE_CASE.

python

```python
MAX_CONNECTIONS = 100
```

9.4.2 Write Modular Code

Break down your code into reusable and independent modules or functions. This enhances readability and facilitates testing.

Example:

python

```python
# Instead of one large function
def process_data():
    # Load data
    # Clean data
    # Analyze data
    # Visualize data
    pass


# Use modular functions
def load_data(filepath):
    pass
```

```python
def clean_data(data):

    pass


def analyze_data(cleaned_data):

    pass


def visualize_data(analysis_results):

    pass
```

9.4.3 Use Docstrings and Comments

Provide clear documentation for your code to explain the purpose and functionality of modules, classes, and functions.

Example:

python

```python
def add(a, b):
    """

    Adds two numbers and returns the result.


    Parameters:

    a (int or float): The first number.

    b (int or float): The second number.
```

Returns:

int or float: The sum of a and b.

"""

return a + b

Pros:

- Enhances understanding for others and your future self.

- Facilitates automatic documentation generation.

9.4.4 Adhere to PEP 8 Style Guide

PEP 8 is Python's official style guide that promotes code consistency and readability.

Key Guidelines:

- **Indentation**: Use four spaces per indentation level.

- **Line Length**: Limit lines to 79 characters.

- **Blank Lines**: Use blank lines to separate functions and classes.

- **Imports**: Place all imports at the top of the file, grouped and ordered appropriately.

- **Whitespace**: Avoid unnecessary whitespace.

python

```
# Correct Import Order
```

```python
import os

import sys


from flask import Flask, render_template
```

9.4.5 Handle Exceptions Gracefully

Use try-except blocks to manage potential errors without crashing your program.

Example:

python

```python
def read_file(filepath):
    try:
        with open(filepath, 'r') as file:
            data = file.read()
        return data
    except FileNotFoundError:
        print(f"Error: The file {filepath} does not exist.")
    except Exception as e:
        print(f"An unexpected error occurred: {e}")
```

Pros:

- Improves program robustness.
- Provides meaningful error messages to users.

9.4.6 Write Unit Tests

Testing ensures that individual units of code work as intended, reducing bugs and facilitating maintenance.

Example: Using unittest

python

```python
import unittest


def multiply(a, b):
    return a * b


class TestMultiply(unittest.TestCase):

    def test_positive_numbers(self):
        self.assertEqual(multiply(3, 4), 12)

    def test_negative_numbers(self):
        self.assertEqual(multiply(-2, -5), 10)

    def test_zero(self):
        self.assertEqual(multiply(0, 5), 0)
```

```
if __name__ == '__main__':

    unittest.main()
```

Pros:

- Detects bugs early in the development process.

- Facilitates code refactoring with confidence.

9.4.7 Use Version Control

Employ version control systems like **Git** to track changes, collaborate with others, and manage different versions of your code.

Example: Basic Git Workflow

1. **Initialize Git Repository**:

bash

```
git init
```

2. **Add Files**:

bash

```
git add .
```

3. **Commit Changes**:

bash

```
git commit -m "Initial commit"
```

4. **Push to Remote Repository**:

bash

```
git remote add origin
https://github.com/username/repo.git

git push -u origin master
```

Pros:

- Maintains a history of changes.
- Facilitates collaboration and code sharing.

Chapter 10: Next Steps and Resources

Congratulations on reaching **Chapter 10: Next Steps and Resources**! By now, you've built a solid foundation in Python programming, tackled various projects, and navigated through common challenges. As you continue your learning journey, it's essential to leverage the right resources, engage with the coding community, and showcase your skills effectively. This chapter provides guidance on how to further enhance your Python expertise, recommended books and courses, ways to join coding communities, and strategies for building a compelling portfolio. Let's explore these avenues to propel your programming career forward!

10.1 Continuing Your Learning Journey

Learning Python is an ongoing process, and there's always more to discover. To continue advancing your skills, consider the following strategies:

10.1.1 Set Clear Goals

Define what you want to achieve with Python. Whether it's web development, data science, automation, or another field, having clear objectives helps you focus your learning efforts.

Examples:

- **Web Development**: Aim to build complex web applications using frameworks like Django or Flask.

- **Data Science**: Focus on mastering libraries such as Pandas, NumPy, and TensorFlow.

- **Automation**: Learn to automate repetitive tasks using Python scripts.

10.1.2 Practice Regularly

Consistent practice is key to retaining and improving your skills. Allocate dedicated time each day or week to code, experiment, and work on projects.

Suggestions:

- **Coding Challenges**: Participate in platforms like LeetCode, HackerRank, or Codewars to solve problems and enhance your problem-solving abilities.

- **Personal Projects**: Develop projects that interest you, such as a personal blog, a game, or a data analysis tool.

10.1.3 Explore Advanced Topics

Delve deeper into specialized areas of Python to expand your knowledge and capabilities.

Advanced Topics:

- **Asynchronous Programming**: Learn about asyncio and asynchronous frameworks to handle concurrent tasks efficiently.

- **Decorators and Generators**: Master these advanced Python features to write more elegant and efficient code.

- **Metaprogramming**: Explore how Python can modify its own behavior at runtime.

10.1.4 Contribute to Open Source

Contributing to open-source projects is an excellent way to gain real-world experience, collaborate with other developers, and build a reputation in the community.

How to Get Started:

- **Find Projects**: Browse repositories on GitHub or GitLab that align with your interests.

- **Start Small**: Begin by fixing bugs, improving documentation, or adding minor features.

- **Engage with Maintainers**: Communicate effectively with project maintainers to understand their needs and guidelines.

10.1.5 Stay Updated

The Python ecosystem is continually evolving with new libraries, frameworks, and best practices. Stay informed to keep your skills relevant.

Ways to Stay Updated:

- **Blogs and Newsletters**: Follow blogs like Real Python and subscribe to newsletters such as Python Weekly.

- **Podcasts**: Listen to podcasts like Talk Python To Me or Python Bytes.

- **Conferences and Meetups**: Attend events like PyCon or local Python meetups to learn from experts and network with peers.

10.2 Recommended Books and Online Courses

Enhance your Python knowledge by leveraging high-quality books and online courses. Here's a curated list to guide your learning:

10.2.1 Recommended Books

1. **"Automate the Boring Stuff with Python" by Al Sweigart**

   - **Description**: Ideal for beginners, this book teaches Python through practical projects like automating tasks, web scraping, and working with Excel files.

   - **Link**: Automate the Boring Stuff

2. **"Python Crash Course" by Eric Matthes**

   - **Description**: A hands-on, project-based introduction to Python, covering fundamental concepts and leading into projects like a simple video game and web applications.

- o **Link**: Python Crash Course

3. **"Fluent Python" by Luciano Ramalho**

- o **Description**: Geared towards intermediate to advanced Python programmers, this book delves into Python's best features and libraries.

- o **Link**: Fluent Python

4. **"Effective Python: 90 Specific Ways to Write Better Python" by Brett Slatkin**

- o **Description**: Offers actionable advice and best practices to improve your Python code, focusing on writing more efficient and readable programs.

- o **Link**: Effective Python

5. **"Python Data Science Handbook" by Jake VanderPlas**

- o **Description**: Comprehensive guide to essential data science libraries in Python, including NumPy, Pandas, Matplotlib, Scikit-Learn, and more.

- o **Link**: Python Data Science Handbook

10.2.2 Recommended Online Courses

1. **Coursera: "Python for Everybody" by University of Michigan**

- Description: A beginner-friendly course covering the basics of Python, data structures, web scraping, and databases.

- Link: Python for Everybody

2. **Udemy: "Complete Python Bootcamp: Go from Zero to Hero in Python 3" by Jose Portilla**

   - Description: Comprehensive course covering Python basics to advanced topics, including decorators, generators, and web scraping.

   - Link: Complete Python Bootcamp

3. **edX: "Introduction to Computer Science and Programming Using Python" by MIT**

   - Description: Rigorous introduction to computer science concepts using Python, suitable for those with some programming experience.

   - Link: MIT's Python Course

4. **DataCamp: "Data Scientist with Python" Career Track**

   - Description: Series of courses focusing on data manipulation, visualization, machine learning, and real-world projects using Python.

   - Link: Data Scientist with Python

5. **Pluralsight: "Advanced Python" by Robert Smallshire**

   - **Description**: For those looking to deepen their Python knowledge, covering advanced topics like metaclasses, decorators, and context managers.

   - **Link**: Advanced Python

10.2.3 Interactive Platforms

1. **Codecademy**

   - **Description**: Offers interactive Python courses with hands-on exercises and projects.

   - **Link**: Codecademy Python

2. **freeCodeCamp**

   - **Description**: Free resources and tutorials covering Python fundamentals and practical projects.

   - **Link**: freeCodeCamp Python

3. **Kaggle Learn**

   - **Description**: Bite-sized tutorials and exercises focused on data science and machine learning with Python.

   - **Link**: Kaggle Learn Python

10.3 Joining Coding Communities

Engaging with coding communities can significantly enhance your learning experience. These communities offer support, resources, networking opportunities, and collaborative projects.

10.3.1 Online Forums and Discussion Boards

1. **Stack Overflow**

   - **Description**: A vast Q&A platform where you can ask questions, share knowledge, and find solutions to programming challenges.

   - **Link**: Stack Overflow Python

2. **Reddit: r/Python**

   - **Description**: A subreddit dedicated to Python news, projects, questions, and discussions.

   - **Link**: r/Python

3. **Dev.to**

   - **Description**: A community of developers sharing articles, tutorials, and insights on Python and other technologies.

   - **Link**: Dev.to Python

4. **Python.org Community Forums**

- o **Description**: Official forums for Python enthusiasts to discuss various topics related to Python programming.
- o **Link**: Python.org Forums

10.3.2 Local Meetups and Conferences

1. **PyCon**

   - o **Description**: The largest annual gathering for the Python community, featuring talks, tutorials, and networking opportunities.
   - o **Link**: PyCon

2. **Local Python Meetups**

   - o **Description**: Join local Python meetups through platforms like Meetup.com to connect with nearby developers.
   - o **Link**: Python Meetups

3. **DjangoCon, FlaskCon, etc.**

   - o **Description**: Conferences focused on specific Python frameworks, offering in-depth talks and workshops.
   - o **Link**: DjangoCon, FlaskCon

10.3.3 Social Media and Networking

1. **Twitter**

   - o **Description**: Follow Python developers, influencers, and organizations to stay updated with the latest trends and discussions.

- o **Hashtags**: #Python, #PyCon, #Django, #Flask

2. **LinkedIn**

   - o **Description**: Connect with professionals, join Python-related groups, and participate in discussions.

   - o **Groups**: Python Developers, Data Science Python

3. **Discord and Slack Channels**

   - o **Description**: Join real-time chat platforms dedicated to Python programming for instant support and collaboration.

   - o **Examples**:

     - ▪ Python Discord

     - ▪ Real Python Community

10.3.4 Contributing to Open Source

1. **GitHub**

   - o **Description**: Explore and contribute to open-source Python projects. Contributing helps you gain experience, collaborate with others, and build your reputation.

   - o **How to Start**:

- **Find Projects**: Look for repositories labeled with good first issue or help wanted.

- **Fork and Clone**: Fork the repository, clone it locally, and start contributing.

- **Submit Pull Requests**: Propose changes by submitting pull requests and engaging with maintainers.

2. **Open Source Initiatives**

   - **Description**: Participate in initiatives like Google Summer of Code or Hacktoberfest to contribute to open-source projects and earn rewards.

10.4 Building a Portfolio

A strong portfolio showcases your skills, projects, and accomplishments to potential employers, clients, or collaborators. Here's how to build an impressive Python portfolio:

10.4.1 Select Your Best Projects

Choose projects that demonstrate a range of your skills and interests. Include projects that solve real-world problems, utilize different libraries or frameworks, and showcase your creativity.

Examples:

- **Data Analysis**: Analyzing a dataset to uncover insights using Pandas and visualization libraries.

- **Web Application**: A Flask or Django-based web app with user authentication and database integration.

- **Game Development**: A simple game built with Pygame.

- **Machine Learning**: A predictive model using Scikit-Learn or TensorFlow.

10.4.2 Use Version Control

Host your projects on platforms like **GitHub** or **GitLab**. This not only provides a backup but also demonstrates your ability to use version control systems effectively.

Tips:

- **Organize Repositories**: Structure your repositories with clear README files, proper folder structures, and descriptive commit messages.

- **Include Documentation**: Provide comprehensive documentation to explain your projects, including setup instructions, usage guides, and feature descriptions.

10.4.3 Create a Personal Website

Having a personal website serves as a centralized hub for your portfolio, resume, blog, and contact information.

How to Create:

- **Static Site Generators**: Use tools like Jekyll, Hugo, or Pelican to build static websites.

- **Web Frameworks**: Develop a custom website using Flask or Django for more dynamic features.

- **Website Builders**: Utilize platforms like Wix, Squarespace, or WordPress if you prefer a less hands-on approach.

Content to Include:

- **About Me**: Share your background, interests, and what drives you as a developer.

- **Portfolio**: Showcase your projects with descriptions, technologies used, and links to live demos or repositories.

- **Blog**: Write articles about your learning experiences, project walkthroughs, or Python tips.

- **Contact Information**: Provide ways for visitors to reach out to you, such as email or social media links.

10.4.4 Highlight Your Skills and Experience

Clearly list the programming languages, frameworks, libraries, and tools you are proficient in. Include any relevant certifications, courses, or achievements.

Examples:

- **Languages**: Python, JavaScript, SQL

- **Frameworks**: Flask, Django, React

- **Libraries**: Pandas, NumPy, Scikit-Learn, TensorFlow

- **Tools**: Git, Docker, Jupyter Notebook

10.4.5 Showcase Testimonials and Recommendations

If you've worked on collaborative projects or contributed to open-source, include testimonials or recommendations from team members, mentors, or project maintainers.

How to Include:

- **LinkedIn Recommendations**: Link to your LinkedIn profile where others have endorsed your skills.

- **Project Readmes**: Add sections in your project READMEs with acknowledgments or quotes from collaborators.

10.4.6 Keep Your Portfolio Updated

Regularly update your portfolio with new projects, skills, and experiences. An up-to-date portfolio reflects your ongoing growth and commitment to learning.

Tips:

- **Add New Projects**: Continuously incorporate recent projects that highlight your latest skills and interests.

- **Update Content**: Refresh your resume, about me section, and project descriptions to align with your current goals.

- **Remove Outdated Work**: If certain projects no longer represent your skill level or interests, consider removing or archiving them.

10.4.7 Optimize for SEO and User Experience

Ensure your portfolio website is easily discoverable and provides a pleasant experience for visitors.

Strategies:

- **Search Engine Optimization (SEO)**: Use relevant keywords, meta descriptions, and alt tags for images to improve your site's visibility on search engines.

- **Responsive Design**: Make sure your website looks and functions well on various devices, including desktops, tablets, and smartphones.

- **Fast Load Times**: Optimize images and use efficient coding practices to ensure your website loads quickly.

10.4.8 Leverage Social Proof

Display metrics or badges that demonstrate your involvement and success in the coding community.

Examples:

- **GitHub Stats**: Embed your GitHub statistics to showcase your contributions.

- **Certifications**: Display badges from completed courses or certifications.

- **Awards**: Highlight any awards or recognitions you've received.

Summary

In **Chapter 10: Next Steps and Resources**, you've explored essential strategies and resources to continue advancing your Python programming journey. Here's a recap of the key areas covered:

- **Continuing Your Learning Journey**: Set clear goals, practice regularly, explore advanced topics, contribute to open source, and stay updated with the latest Python developments.

- **Recommended Books and Online Courses**: Leveraged a curated list of books and online courses to deepen your Python knowledge and skills across various domains.

- **Joining Coding Communities**: Engaged with online forums, local meetups, social media platforms, and open-source projects to connect with other developers, seek support, and collaborate on projects.

- **Building a Portfolio**: Learned how to select and showcase your best projects, utilize version control, create a personal website, highlight your skills, and maintain an up-to-date and optimized portfolio to impress potential employers or clients.

Next Steps:

1. **Implement the Strategies**: Apply the learning strategies and resources mentioned to structure your ongoing education and project development.

2. **Engage Actively**: Participate in coding communities, contribute to open-source projects, and seek feedback to enhance your skills and visibility.

3. **Showcase Your Work**: Develop and maintain a professional portfolio that effectively demonstrates your capabilities, projects, and growth as a Python developer.

4. **Pursue Specializations**: As you gain confidence, consider specializing in areas like data science, web development, automation, or machine learning to carve out a niche in the job market.

Recommended Resources:

- **GitHub**: https://github.com/ - Host and collaborate on projects.

- **Stack Overflow**: https://stackoverflow.com/ - Seek answers to programming questions.

- **Reddit: r/Python**: https://www.reddit.com/r/Python/ - Join discussions and stay updated.

- **Real Python**: https://realpython.com/ - Access tutorials, articles, and resources.

- **Kaggle**: https://www.kaggle.com/ - Participate in data science competitions and projects.

By embracing these next steps and utilizing the recommended resources, you'll continue to grow as a proficient Python developer, ready to tackle more complex challenges and seize exciting opportunities in the tech landscape. Keep pushing your boundaries, stay curious, and enjoy the endless possibilities that Python programming offers. Happy coding!

www.ingramcontent.com/pod-product-compliance
Lightning Source LLC
LaVergne TN
LVHW022333060326
832902LV00022B/4015